MW00736852

GOD MARRIAGE & MONEY

Discovering Your Money Mindsets

God Marriage & Money

Discovering Your Money Mindsets

Published by Compass Catholic Ministries

Copyright © 2014 by Compass Catholic Ministries. All Rights Reserved.

Scripture texts in this work are taken from the *New American Bible with Revised New Testament and Revised Psalms* © 1991, 1986, 1970 Confraternity of Christian Doctrine, Washington, D.C. and are used by permission of the copyright owner. All Rights Reserved. No part of the New American Bible may be reproduced in any form without permission in writing from the copyright owner.

English translation of the *Catechism of the Catholic Church* for the United States of America Copyright © 1994, United States Catholic Conference, Inc.— Libreria Editrice Vaticana. English translation of the: Catechism of the Catholic Church Modifications from the Editio Typica Copyright © 1997, United States Catholic Conference, Inc.—Libreria Editrice Vaticana. Used with permission.

Excerpts from *Stewardship: A Disciple's Response* Copyright © 2002 United States Conference of Catholic Bishops, Washington D.C. Used with permission. All rights reserved. No part of this work may be reproduced or transmitted in any form without the permission in writing from the copyright holder.

Excerpts from *United States Catholic Catechism for Adults* Copyright © 2006 United States Conference of Catholic Bishops, Washington D.C. Used with permission. All rights reserved. No part of this work may be reproduced or transmitted in any form without the permission in writing from the copyright holder.

ISBN 978-0-9910540-2-2

Printed in the United States of America

This book is dedicated to our brothers and sisters in Christ.

To those of you who have supported Compass Catholic Ministries through your prayers, encouraging words, advice, volunteer efforts and donations, we are grateful that you are a part of our lives and we appreciate you more than we can express.

To those of you meeting Compass Catholic Ministries for the first time through this book, we pray that your married lives will be enriched as you work together on your faith and finances. May God richly bless your life together.

We pray that your interaction with Compass Catholic Ministries will be one small step in a long and faith filled life journey for all of you.

Table Of Contents

Introduction	7
A Tale of Two Couples	9
A Three-Ply Cord	17
We are Stewards	23
Will You be Honest or Truthful?	27
Our Culture	33
Making Wise Decisions	39
Plan Your Foundation	45
Giving	51
The Detailed Spending Plan	57
Crisis	67
Debt	75
Know Your Credit Score	85
Major Purchases	91
Saving and Investing	103
Children	111
Estate Planning	119
Forever	125
Resources	129
Bible References	130
Financial Dictionary	134

Introduction

Communication is usually the number one issue in a marriage and one of the most difficult things to talk about can be money. It's sad to say that before the wedding many couples spend more time talking about the flavor of their wedding cake than about their joint finances. The cake cutting ritual at a wedding usually takes less than 10 minutes. Yet finances are something they will deal with on a day-to-day basis for the rest of their lives!

Misunderstandings about finances can often be the trigger for arguments, tension, anger and even divorce; and the divorce rate for Christians is no different than the divorce rate for the general population.

This workbook defines ways to deal with money that are important for engaged couples to learn. The principles in this workbook are based on the Bible and Catholic teaching.

Each chapter of the book discusses a specific topic related to money in marriage. At the end of each chapter there is an Insight, a Bible reference and a quote from a Catholic source that sum up the chapter. The "Connect" section provides a series of questions and activities to help you and your fiancé thoroughly discuss how you will manage money as a couple. These questions will help you work together to discover and resolve differing attitudes about finances that will impact your marriage.

At the end of the section, there is a "Prayer Intention" heading where you will find a blank space to write a prayer intention for your marriage, related to the specific topic of the chapter.

The way you handle money and your attitudes towards possessions can unite or divide you as a couple. We pray that this small workbook will bring you many blessings and help you learn to handle money in ways that honor God and bring you closer together as a couple.

Chapter One
A Tale of Two Couples

When people enter into a marriage, they bring to it all the assumptions and experiences of their families in the way they use and manage money. Each spouse was raised in a different environment so no two people come into a marriage thinking exactly the same way as their spouse on any issue, most especially money.

Maybe one of you was raised in a family where debt was the norm, or maybe you were raised in a family that always paid cash for everything. Maybe your parents gave you a generous spending allowance, or maybe you had to earn every penny you spent starting at an early age. Maybe your parents gave you a credit card, or maybe they helped you develop a budget.

> A wedding is a day; a marriage is a lifetime!

No matter what your background is, the way each of you handles money needs to be discussed and understood by both of you, or it will become an issue in your marriage. Reportedly, fifty percent of marriages end in divorce and, many times, money is the root cause of the conflict. It is important for you to develop a way to discuss and manage money in your marriage—not just when bills are due, or when the debt is overwhelming, or when a large purchase needs to be made, but everyday. If you develop a foundation for managing money in your marriage, you can prevent many future problems. The ability to communicate well about money will strengthen your communication in other areas as well.

It is equally important that the husband and wife share responsibility for the analysis and decision making related to marital finances. This is true whether one or both spouses work, no matter who has the larger income or who actually functions as the family accountant. Finances are a shared responsibility.

All couples will have differences of opinion about money at some point in their marriage. Couples who have successful marriages have figured out how to talk about money, and how to resolve differences of opinion by working through them together.

What follows is the story of two couples who recently married and had to quickly learn how to discuss finances in their marriage.

Couple One each had good jobs that paid well. They were able to save a substantial amount of money before they got married and they bought a nice house before the wedding. After the wedding, they moved into the house, and were able to furnish and decorate it. Since their income was generous, they were also able to spend without restrictions and enjoyed traveling, eating out and taking nice vacations.

Couple Two ran into money problems before the wedding when the wife lost her job. She could no longer afford the rent on her apartment, so she moved back home with her parents. Shortly after the wedding, the husband lost his job so he also moved in with his wife's parents. Because they had no source of income, they used credit card cash advances for the money they needed on a daily basis.

What happened to these two couples?

Couple One was doing so well that the wife decided to quit her job and open her own business with a friend as her partner. The business thrived for about a year, then quickly folded. Once she started her business, their income was cut by more than half. They never changed their lifestyle and they continued to buy things, go places and enjoy entertainment activities using their credit cards.

Because of the increased debt, the husband took a temporary job assignment halfway across the country. He was only able to travel home once a month. The wife could not find another job in her field, and refused to take a job unless it was in her specific field. Because of their credit card debt, it was not possible for her to travel to her husband's location. On the weekends when the husband did come home, he found the bills waiting for him to pay, all the maintenance items around the house waiting for him to do and an unhappy wife who was keeping herself busy by buying things and going places. Each time he was home they had discussions about cutting back on spending and her plan to get any job to bring in some extra money, but nothing ever changed. They are now divorced.

Couple Two also had their challenges. They had a hard time finding jobs in their fields and the lack of income was supplemented by credit card spending. They hated being married and living with her parents, but they could not rent an apartment due to the debt they had accumulated. They vowed to change their circumstances and decided to take any jobs they could find in order to save and pay down their debt so they could move into their own place. They prayed for guidance and strength. After several months of hard work, and much prayer, they paid down their credit cards and saved enough money to move into their own apartment. They were finally able to find employment in their fields. Because of all their debt, they both decided to keep their part time jobs to earn extra income. They used the extra income to pay off their debt and they are now saving to buy a house.

What made the difference?

Couple One had such a good financial position in the beginning that they never talked about money, thinking they would always have enough to do what they wanted to do. When the wife started her business, they never sat down to figure out the impact to their finances if the business was unsuccessful. Because of their lack of communication, when trouble hit they played the "blame game" pointing fingers at each other. They each thought their problems would be solved if only the other person would change. Since they had no framework for working out their problems, each subsequent issue put their relationship into a faster downward spiral.

Couple Two also had to learn how to communicate about money, but they made the effort to learn how to work through their issues together. They had open communication, and did not play the "blame game." Praying together helped them focus on the issues in front of them and brought them closer together. They worked together to develop a plan they both agreed with, and they encouraged each other to stick to the plan.

Chapter One

The question is which couple will you be?

Insights

You both bring preconceived notions, and attitudes learned from your families into your marriage. In a successful marriage you recognize your own strengths and your own weaknesses. You also learn to recognize and honor your spouse's strengths and weaknesses. For example a strength can be that one of you is very detail oriented and may balance their checkbook to the penny each month. A weakness can be that one of you likes to shop when stressed out by work. This knowledge, if shared and openly discussed with each other, will allow you to work together to make plans, and openly acknowledge and solve any issues.

The Bible says

"Two are better than one: They get a good wage for their toil. If the one falls, the other will help the fallen one. But woe to the solitary person! If that one should fall, there is no other to help. Where one alone may be overcome, two together can resist. A three-ply cord is not easily broken." (Ecclesiastes 4:9,10,12)

Catholicism

"Marriage is based on the consent of the contracting parties, that is, on their will to give themselves, each to the other, mutually and definitively, in order to live a covenant of faithful and fruitful love." (*Catechism of the Catholic Church*, 1662)

Connect

1. Do you and your fiancé pray together? If not, why not?

2. List three of your financial strengths and three of your financial weaknesses. Share with your fiancé.

3. How are you and your fiancé alike in how you handle money and how are you different?

4. Discuss what you think your biggest challenge will be regarding money in your marriage.

5. What is the biggest adjustment you'll have to make financially after the wedding?

Prayer Intention

Chapter 2

A Three-Ply Cord

The Bible verse from Ecclesiastes at the end of Chapter One referred to a three-ply cord. In marriage, this three-ply cord is God, you and your spouse. Most people do not think that God has anything to do with their finances and they are astounded to find that there are over 2,500 verses in the Bible that relate to money and possessions. There are fewer than 500 verses on prayer and about 500 verses on faith. More than half of the parables are related to money and fifteen percent of everything Jesus said had to do with money.

Why does the Bible say so much about money? Probably because God knew how much we would deal with money and how tempting it is for us to misuse it. Think about how much time you spend on a daily basis making money, spending money or using something you bought with money—almost 100 percent of our time is somehow related to money. It is imperative that we know how to use money wisely according to God's financial principles.

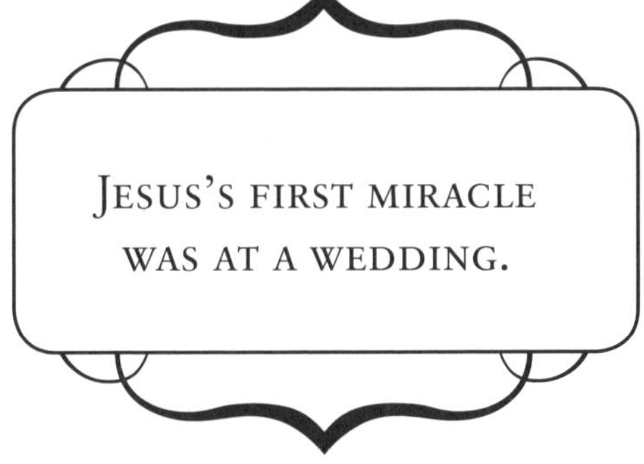

Just as you and your spouse have a role to play in how you manage money, God also has a role. He is the owner of everything and will provide for your needs. If the Lord can feed 5,000 with only two fish and five loaves of bread, he can also meet your needs.

The challenge is that our culture tells us that we can provide for our own needs and that we own what we possess. In reality, we own nothing; all we possess is a blessing from God. In Genesis 1:28, God said to Adam and Eve, "Have dominion over the fish of the sea, the birds of the air, and all the living things that crawl on the earth." Note that God gave them dominion over the earth and the beasts on it—not ownership. In reality we own nothing.

It is hard for us to recognize God's ownership, as he is invisible to us. Yet, when we do learn this principle, it leads to great peace and contentment.

God is faithful! He made everything—just think about all that he has done for us. We really do know deep down inside that everything comes from God, we just do not live that way. Nothing in the American culture encourages us to live in a way that acknowledges God.

However, money can be the lever to our hearts. Money can be what draws us closer to God or what drives us to put up a wall between God and ourselves. So many times, we hold on to our money as if it were more important to us than God, but using money wisely and with the right attitude will bring you many blessings.

God can bless us with supply—maybe you are so wealthy that your wealth can be used to build up God's kingdom here on earth. Or God can bless us by withholding—as we struggle together in tough financial situations, it can make our marriage stronger. Money can reveal our need for God—sometimes we are in such a bad place financially that all we are able to do is depend on him.

Money can clarify our values as we face temptations and challenges. When we give, save and spend in a manner pleasing to God we can grow closer as a couple, then together grow closer to God. We must decide which is more important to us—money or God?

Insights

Larry Burkett, a Christian author, once wrote, "When we acknowledge God's ownership, every spending decision becomes a spiritual decision. No longer do we ask 'Lord what do you want me to do with my money?' The question is restated 'Lord, what do you want me to do with your money?' When we have this perspective, spending and saving decisions are equally as spiritual as giving decisions."

The Bible says

"Yours, LORD, are greatness and might, majesty, victory, and splendor. For all in heaven and on earth is yours; yours, LORD, is kingship; you are exalted as head over all. Riches and glory are from you, and you have dominion over all. In your hand are power and might; it is yours to give greatness and strength to all." (1 Chronicles 29:11-12)

"Look, the heavens, even the highest heavens, belong to the LORD, your God, as well as the earth and everything on it." (Deuteronomy 10:14)

"'Mine is the silver and mine the gold—Oracle of the Lord of Hosts." (Haggai 2:8)

"For every animal of the forest is mine, beasts by the thousands on my mountains. I know every bird in the heights; whatever moves in the wild is mine." (Psalm 50:10-11)

Catholicism

"How can I ever express the happiness of a marriage joined by the Church, strengthened by an offering, sealed by a blessing, announced by angels, and ratified by the Father?... How wonderful the bond between two believers, now one in hope, one in desire, one in discipline, one in the same service! They are both children of one Father and servants of the same Master, undivided in spirit and flesh, truly two in one flesh. Where the flesh is one, one also is the spirit." (Tertullian, ecclesiastical writer)

Connect

1. What are some ways you can recognize God's ownership? In what ways do you think this "change of heart" would change your outlook?

2. What does the word "dominion" mean to you and how is it different than "ownership"?

3. Discuss the sentence "We will use money properly in our marriage." What does that phrase mean to you?

Prayer Intention

Chapter 3
We are Stewards

If God is the owner of everything, "steward" is the word that best describes our role. A steward is a person who protects and cares for the land, property or money of another. If we truly believe that God owns everything, then our role while we are here on earth is to be a steward of all the blessings he has given us.

There are many areas in which we are called to be stewards. The Sacrament of Marriage calls us to be stewards of the relationship with our spouse and never take that relationship for granted. Children are a gift from God and we must care for them and love them. Our faith is a gift and we are called to be stewards of our faith. All of these things, and many more, are gifts from God and you must tend these gifts carefully and gratefully.

As a steward, you are also called to take care of the material blessings in your life and be grateful to God for giving them to you. Being a steward means recognizing that none of the material items in your possession are permanent. The things in this world are temporary—how many times have you seen a U-Haul on the back end of a hearse? Too often we live like we will be in this world forever. After all, the world we inhabit is one that appears to be real; it is what we see, feel, hear, taste and smell. It is easy to forget that this world is temporary and our life after this world is everlasting.

Philippians 3:20 tells us "Our citizenship is in heaven" not earth. We are aliens, strangers, and pilgrims on earth. Peter wrote, "conduct yourselves with reverence during the time of your sojourning" (1 Peter 1:17). 1 Chronicles 29:15 reminds us, "For before you we are strangers and travelers, like all our ancestors. Our days on earth are like a shadow, without a future." We are to be pilgrims, aliens and strangers in this world—our real home is in heaven. In light of eternity, we are only here for a short time.

Pilgrims are unattached. Material things are only valuable to the extent that they facilitate the journey. Things can entrench us in the present world, acting as chains around our legs that keep us from moving in response to God. When our eyes are too focused on the visible, they will be drawn away from the invisible. "We look not to what is seen but to what is unseen; for what is seen is transitory, but what is unseen is eternal" (2 Corinthians 4:18).

As real as this world seems, it's not where we belong. Our real future begins at the end of our pilgrimage. Pilgrims of faith look to the next world. They see earthly possessions for what they are: useful for kingdom purposes, but far too flimsy to bear the weight of trust. Fr. Leo Trese, author of *The Faith Explained*, says it this way, "Wiser people know that worldly well-being is a deceptive source of happiness… [they] have discovered that there is no happiness so deep and so abiding as that which grows out of a living faith in God, and an active, fruitful love for God."

Chapter 3

Insights

As a steward, we will one day be accountable to the owner (God) for how we managed what he has entrusted to us. We must be faithful managers with even the smallest things, and we must be faithful in every area of our lives.

The Bible says

"What profit would there be for one to gain the whole world and forfeit his life." (Matthew 16:26)

"If therefore, you are not trustworthy with dishonest wealth, who will trust you with true wealth?" (Luke 16:11)

Catholicism

"In his use of things man should regard the external goods he legitimately owns not merely as exclusive to himself but common to others also, in the sense that they can benefit others as well as himself. The ownership of any property makes its holder a steward of Providence, with the task of making it fruitful and communicating its benefits to others, first of all his family." (*Catechism of the Catholic Church* 2404)

Connect

1. What does it mean to you to be a pilgrim in this world?

We are Stewards

2. Discuss your role as a steward and what it means to your marriage.

3. Why is it so hard to realize that things of this world are temporary?

4. What are some practical ideas for recognizing your role as a steward?

Prayer Intention

Chapter 4
Will You be Honest or Truthful?

Pretend you have just received a windfall of $1,000,000. As a couple, discuss what you would do with that much money.

After the discussion, step back a little and rethink what you were just talking about. Did each of you openly and honestly express your opinion? Did you find a way to iron out your differences? Or did one of you simply agree with the other to keep the peace?

Sometimes, when there is a difference of opinion, people tell little white lies about money to avoid conflict. If you found yourself doing that in this exercise, or if you have done it in the past, then there may be bigger issues in your relationship than little white lies about money.

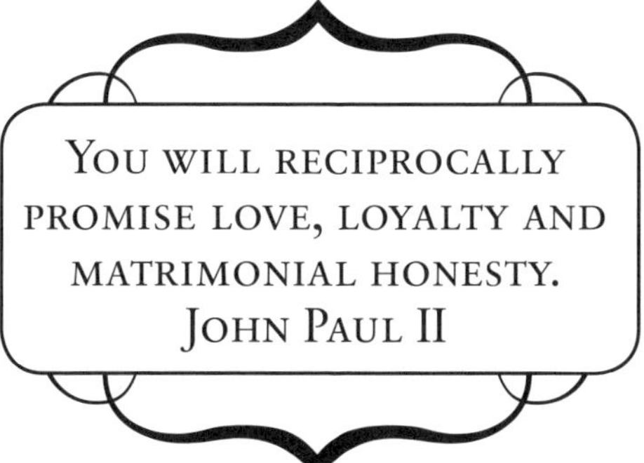

Fifty or sixty years ago, if you had asked someone if they were honest or truthful, they would have looked at you as if you had two heads. At that time, there was no discernable difference between the two. Our attitudes have changed so much that today people often manipulate their words and actions so they are scrupulously truthful without being absolutely honest. Unfortunately, the act of being totally truthful without being absolutely honest is acceptable in our secular society.

Will You be Honest or Truthful?

Judges 17:6 reads, "In those days there was no king in Israel; everyone did what was right in their own eyes." When we act in ways acceptable to the secular world, but unacceptable in our spiritual lives, we are acting as if our living King, Jesus Christ, is incapable of discovering our dishonesty and disciplining us.

Think of the Pharisees who were utterly meticulous in giving their tithe. They even made sure to include the smallest mint leaf in their offering. But they were giving their offerings from a sense of duty rather than a sense of love and their attitude was not pleasing to God.

It is human nature to try and avoid the feelings of fright or discomfort, yet acting dishonestly is never an acceptable way to make ourselves feel better. When we act dishonestly, we take matters into our own hands and manipulate situations to our benefit.

By manipulating our actions and words to be totally truthful without being honest, or by telling "little white lies" to avoid conflict, we are just as displeasing to God as the Pharisees. Society's acceptance of relative honesty is the opposite of what we learn in Scripture. The Lord requires absolute honesty from all of us at all times in every aspect of our life.

All of us make many small decisions about being honest every day. Do you deal honestly in all areas of your life, even the smallest ones? Or do you quietly smile and pocket the extra money if the cashier makes a mistake when giving you change? Have you ever sold something and not been entirely truthful because you may have lost the sale? Do you cheat on your taxes —even just a little? Do you bring supplies home from the office for personal use?

Chapter 4

When we act dishonestly we are deceiving another person. We may fool ourselves into thinking it's just a business, or the government, or an insurance company. We may talk ourselves into thinking we are just trying to avoid conflict, but the victim is always a person and ultimately it is the business owners, the other consumers, or the taxpayers, or your spouse you are hurting. In these situations, we are directly harming one of God's children.

Our actions speak louder than our words and acting dishonestly dims the light of Christ shining within us, erodes our faith response, and tarnishes the Christian life that others see in us.

A hint of dishonesty may creep into your marriage if you decide to have separate checking or savings accounts to hide your spending from your spouse. While it may be good to have separate accounts so you both have some level of financial accountability be careful that separate accounts are not being used to hide a level of honesty that is required in marriage. Genesis 2:24 says "That is why a man leaves his father and mother and clings to his wife, and the two of them become one body." You are not truly becoming one if you are separating your finances.

Marriage is meant to be a blessing and one of the ways to honor that blessing is to be absolutely open and honest at all times about everything.

Insights

Little white lies are easy to tell, but each one leaves a small chip in the foundation of your marriage and too many small chips will result in a cracked foundation. And if you are lying about money, then your spouse has every right to wonder what else you may be lying about.

Will You be Honest or Truthful?

The Bible says

"Scoundrels, villains, are they who deal in crooked talk." (Proverbs 6:12)

"Lying lips are an abomination to the Lord, but those who are truthful, his delight." (Proverbs 12:22)

Catholicism

"By its very nature, lying is to be condemned. It is a profanation of speech, whereas the purpose of speech is to communicate known truth to others. The deliberate intention of leading a neighbor into error by saying things contrary to the truth constitutes a failure in justice and charity." (*Catechism of the Catholic Church* 2485)

Connect

1. Go back to the first paragraph of this section. Discuss in an honest and open manner the choices you would make with a $1,000,000 windfall.

2. Will you have joint or separate accounts and what are the reasons for that decision?

3. After questions one and two, talk about the interactions between the two of you when you agreed or disagreed.

4. Determine if there are any ideas for improving the way you communicated during this exercise.

5. Define any assumptions you have about money in your marriage. Share with your fiancé.

Prayer Intention

Chapter 5
Our Culture

We live in a world defined by Madison Avenue. Advertisers tell us that we should get everything we want when we want it because we deserve it. The most popular television shows are reality shows that allow us to put ourselves in the place of the contestants as they vie for big money and exotic trips. If we could only own this or that, have more money or drive that car, then we would finally be happy.

Easy credit can provide whatever we desire. We are influenced to think that having more things means a better life, which leads us to want everything we see. The more we watch TV, surf the net, read magazines and listen to the radio, the more money we spend in an unending quest to be happy. Commercials barrage us with almost non-stop advertising—it's everywhere! We even wear advertising on our clothes.

Yet are these messages really giving us the happiness we crave and can only find in God?

We've lost the ability to distinguish between needs and wants. Needs are food, clothing and shelter. Wants are restaurant meals, the latest fashions, the biggest house and the newest gadgets.

Our culture sends us spinning in cycles of wanting everything and buying things we don't really need. We get into debt for these unnecessary things and the debt causes us worry and stress. To relieve the worry and stress, we buy more stuff, and the cycle continues.

When we fall into this trap, we are focusing our desires and betting our happiness on worldly objects and not on God. We are making these worldly objects our "strange god" and making them more important than God.

Matthew (19:16-30), Mark (10:17-31) and Luke (18:18-30) all contain the parable of the Rich Young Man, where Jesus explains that our attitude towards wealth and possessions is in conflict with where our true focus should be. The young man in the parable has faithfully observed the Commandments and asks Jesus what else he can do to gain eternal life. Like most of us, the young man yearns for life in its fullest. He thinks that he may be able to use his wealth to purchase eternal happiness.

Jesus understands the young man's attitude, his dependence on, and attachment to, his wealth and possessions. Jesus' advice is that he must sell all of his possessions, give his money to the poor and then follow him. In following Jesus' advice, the rich young man's treasure and his heart will no longer be on earth, and he will put God above all else. When the young man heard this, he turned away because he was very rich. He was focused on wealth and temporal happiness as opposed to eternal happiness.

Many of us would probably display the same sentiments as the rich young man. We have many possessions and these possessions are of great importance to us. Like this young man, if Jesus came into our lives today and told us to sell all that we have and give the money to the poor, there is every possibility we would also turn away.

Jesus goes on to tell the disciples, "How hard it is for those who have wealth to enter the kingdom of God." This amazed the disciples and so Jesus goes a little further in his explanation, "For it is easier for a camel to pass through the eye of a needle than for a rich person to enter the kingdom of God."

The problem is not in being rich. In fact there are many rich people in the Bible, such as Abraham, Jacob, Samuel, Job and David, whom God blessed. The problem is our attitude when worldly things become more important to us than God. Society tells us that only things can make us important and bring us true happiness. When we believe this, we forsake God for our possessions.

One of the most misquoted verses in the Bible is 1 Timothy 6:10: "For the love of money is the root of all evils, and some people in their desire for it have strayed from the faith and have pierced themselves with many pains." Money is not evil, it's the love of money which causes problems. Money is simply a tool we use as a medium of exchange. What can be evil is our attitude towards money.

Wealth and possessions will never make us happy for long. A few short days or weeks after we purchase that "must have" item, it becomes just another thing we own and we "must have" something else to fill the void.

Insights

Put your possessions in the proper perspective.

The Bible says

"No one can serve two masters. He will either hate one and love the other, or be devoted to one and despise the other. You cannot serve God and mammon [money}." (Matthew 6:24)

Our Culture

Catholicism

"I still remember my childhood picture Bible, which showed a shiny golden calf with people bowing down before it—a colorful depiction of the idolatry into which the ancient Israelites fell after Moses led them out of Egypt (Ex 32). The story struck me as incredibly strange for two reasons. First, I wondered why anyone would be so ridiculous as to worship a golden calf. Obviously, the gold statue was not really a living god. Second, I wondered why God would care so much about what they did. They weren't hurting anyone (were they?). It may be silly to worship a calf of gold, but why would God be concerned?

As an adult, I know from personal experience that the temptation to worship money rather than God is not limited to ancient Israel. People in our society are unlikely to bow down before a golden calf, but almost everyone in our society is tempted by greed in one of its forms. And, just as with ancient Israel, God cares about whether or not we are greedy." (Christopher Kaczor, *Catholic Answers*, Volume 19 Number 3)

Connect

1. What in our culture influences you the most: TV, internet, magazines, billboards, catalogues, etc.?

2. How much do your friends, neighbors, co-workers and extended family influence your buying habits?

3. What is really important to you when you spend money?

4. How often do you overspend when shopping?

5. How close are your credit cards to being maxed out?

Prayer Intention

Chapter 6

Making Wise Decisions

Everyday we make many spending decisions. Should I take the toll road? Where do I want to go for lunch? What bills need to be paid today?

Before your marriage, you can make your own financial decisions. After marriage, financial decisions must become a joint effort since every financial decision affects both of you. These decisions can be something really important, such as your budget for buying a house, or something as simple as deciding on cooking at home or spending the extra money to eat out.

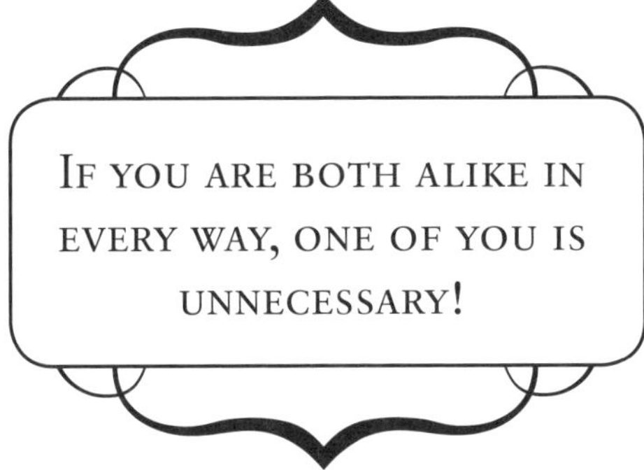

In Paul's discussion of the body of Christ in 1 Corinthians 12:12-31, each of us is pictured as a different member of Christ's body. Our ability to function most effectively is dependent on the members working together. God has given each of us certain abilities and gifts, but God has not given any one person all the abilities that he or she needs to be most productive.

This premise is the same in a marriage. The first person you should talk to about spending money is your spouse. In Chapter One, your "Connect" was to identify your strengths and weaknesses. Most couples find that they have complimentary styles. A weak area for one is a strong area for the other and the strongest marriages use complimentary traits to work as a team. Regardless of your spouse's financial training or education, you need to honor your spouse by considering their position, requesting their input, and taking them seriously. Then both of you should make a decision that is mutually agreeable. When a husband or wife seeks the other's advice, he or she actually is communicating, "I love you. We are partners. I need your perspective."

Just as lying dishonors your spouse, so does making one-sided decisions—where one of you spends in a way that the other person does not agree with. A husband and wife should agree because they both will experience the consequences of the decision. Even if their mutual choice proves to be disastrous, their relationship remains intact. There are no grounds for an "I told you so" response. If the two of you do not agree about a spending decision, then don't do it until you have a chance to talk it out and come to a joint agreement.

Consistently talking to each other also keeps both of you informed about your true financial condition. This knowledge is important in the event you predecease your spouse or are unable to work. Once you understand your fiancé's spending habits, it will be easier for you to counsel each other.

It is also important for both of you to get wise counsel from others. Notice the phrase wise counsel—this does not mean getting counsel from your best friend who will always agree with you. Generally, after your spouse, go to your parents as the first choice for counsel. Parents probably know you better than anyone else and can often bring a perspective that you do not have on your own. But the advice of parents should never be taken if it is in conflict with advice from your spouse.

A second source of wise counsel is like-minded people. If you are following God's principles of managing money, then getting counsel from others who are also following God's principles is a good idea. You can encourage each other and keep each other on track.

Lastly, you can get counsel from a professional. For example, if you are making investment decisions you should seek advice from a professional who is in the financial services business. BUT be cautious and recognize that a professional selling you something has a vested interest in your decision. A car salesman will rarely advise you to wait and buy a car in a few months when you have a bigger down payment. Similarly, a financial advisor may get a larger commission by selling you certain products. You need to understand how a professional gets compensated for their products and/or services before you make a decision to follow their advice.

Insights

After marriage, any financial decisions must become a joint effort since every financial decision affects both of you. You need to agree to agree.

The Bible says

"Yes, excellent advice I give you; my teaching do not forsake." (Proverbs 4:2)

"The way of fools is right in their own eyes, but those who listen to advice are the wise." (Proverbs 12:15)

Catholicism

"The complicated thing about money in a marriage is that it's often tied up with power. We may believe that the person who makes the most money is more valued or should have the greater say in financial decisions. We need to remember that spouses perform many tasks for which they are not paid. They contribute to the marriage and common life in different ways. At times one spouse may be ill or unemployed and not able to contribute financially or in other ways. Spouses need to feel valued and respected in their own home, regardless of how much money they bring in. " (M. Gary Neuman and Melisa Neuman, "Overcoming Obstacles / Finances," *For Your Marriage,* www.foryourmarriage.org)

Connect

One of the first areas where you can seek counsel from each other is deciding on how you will manage money as a couple. Discuss the following:

1. What role will each of you take in the family finances? (Example: Who tracks the spending plan? Who balances the checking account? Who manages the on-line payments?)

2. How often will you discuss finances to be sure you both are up to date on your financial situation?

Chapter 6

3. How much can each of you spend without checking with your spouse first?

4. Discuss people in your lives who would be Godly counselors.

Prayer Intention

Chapter 7

Plan Your Foundation

You've probably heard the saying, "Most people do not plan to fail, they fail to plan." This is very true in the area of managing money. Money can either trickle through your fingers, or you can tell it where to go. The trickle process leaves you with a sense of frustration as you really don't know where the money went and you may have ended up with unfulfilled needs.

As stewards we are required to be trustworthy handling the money God has given us. First Corinthians 4:2 tells us "Now it is of course required of stewards that they be found trustworthy." If you plan and manage your spending, at the end of the month you know exactly where the money went and have a sense of accomplishment not frustration and you have been a trustworthy steward.

The word "budget" has a very negative connotation for most people. It sounds like you can't buy anything, do anything, or go anywhere. It appears restrictive and limiting. In short, a budget does not sound like a lot of fun. But, think about it. A budget simply tells you the amount of money coming in and the amount of money going out. So you do have a budget, whether you realize it or not and whether or not you call it a budget.

Plan Your Foundation

It's similar to a diet. You eat every day, so you do have a diet. What most people mean when they say "diet" is that they want to manage what they eat. Similarly a budget lets you manage what you spend. To make it sound more appealing, instead of a budget, think of it as a "Spending Plan," which sounds like a lot more fun! Having a spending plan lays a strong foundation you can build on, as it will guide you in making fact based decisions.

On a journey, you need to know your starting point. In order to start your spending plan, you have to know your starting point, which is exactly how much money is coming in and going out on a regular basis.

This is a very simple concept and can easily be explained using two finger economics. Hold up the first two fingers of your left hand. Point to the tallest finger … then to the shorter one. The taller finger represents what comes in (income), and the shorter finger represents what goes out (expenses). So money comes in and goes out. And if you ever get the two fingers mixed up and the big one is what goes out and the little one is what comes in, then you are spending more than you make and are in big trouble!

You must know where the money is going if you are to have any hope of managing it. Income is pretty easy to track as most people get paid on a regular basis. However, what is going out can be more difficult to track, because so much of the money we spend simply seems to disappear. Unless you know where your money is going, how do you know if you are spending it on what is most important to both of you?

The starting point is to begin tracking what you are spending every day. The tracking needs to be done in a way both of you can use, and it should not be a burden. During the day you can keep a 3x5 notecard in your pocket or purse and write down what you spend. Another way is to take a picture of the item with your smart phone and note the amount spent. You can also get a receipt for your purchase to help you remember. Each evening enter all the spending for the day in a notebook, budgeting software or spreadsheet. Keep track of the date, amount spent and what you spent it on. Just make sure that you record what was spent so you can understand it, analyze it and manage it. Keep it simple!

Have you ever had $20 in your pocket one day only to find it gone, having no recollection of where it went? Tracking your spending will help you to see where that $20 dollars went. But more importantly, it gives you concrete information so you can decide if you want the money to go to that same place the next time. Until you know where your money is going, you have no hope of managing it.

Many people have had their eyes opened using this process. One person was buying lunches each day at work. He thought he was spending $50-$60 monthly. After tracking his spending, he found he was actually spending over $250 each month, which added up to about $3,000 in a year. It was a real eye opener, as his goal was to save money for a trip to Europe. Tracking his spending allowed him to see that he was spending a lot of money on something that was not important to him. He decided it was much more important to go to Europe instead of going out for lunch at a restaurant.

HERE IS THE MAIN POINT—Until you know how much money you are spending, and where it is going, you don't have enough information to know if you want to continue spending the money that way. By tracking your spending you can be sure the money is going to the places that have the highest priority for both of you. This doesn't stop you from spending, it simply lets you control how and where you are spending money.

Plan Your Foundation

Most people use a big bucket approach to spending. There is one big bucket and all their money goes into the big bucket and if they spend money it comes out of the big bucket. These people often find that at the end of the month there is no money in the bucket. The bucket is empty before the end of the month.

A spending plan is a little bucket approach. Instead of putting all the money into one big bucket, you put the money into a few little buckets, and you define the little buckets and how much money goes into each. For example, your little buckets—or spending categories—may be housing, groceries, utilities, clothes, transportation, debt payment, savings, etc. By creating categories you are defining where the money goes. This approach provides freedom and makes decisions simpler—not more complicated. When the little bucket is empty, then no more money can be spent in that category. After tracking your spending for 60 days (this includes all spending—cash, credit cards, bill payer accounts, etc.), categorize where you spent your money over the previous 60 days. Try it for the next 60 days and see what you learn. Encourage each other and talk about what you are finding out about your spending habits.

Insights

When you develop and use a spending plan, it puts you in control of telling the money where you want it to go.

The Bible says

"According to the grace of God given to me, like a wise master builder I laid a foundation, and another is building upon it. But each one must be careful how he builds upon it, for no one can lay a foundation other than the one that is there, namely, Jesus Christ." (1 Corinthians 3:10)

Catholicism

"Money should serve not rule." (Pope Francis)

Connect

1. List three positive things about using a spending plan.

2. Discuss the best way for you as a couple to track your day-to-day spending.

3. Start your 60-day tracking today!

Prayer Intention

Chapter 8

Giving

Once you have tracked your day-to-day spending for about 60 days, you know where the money is going and you can get to the next level of detail. You know how much comes in and how much is going out. Before diving into details about how much you are spending on yourselves, it's time to look at how much you are giving back to God.

Earlier in this book you were challenged to consider that everything you have is a gift from God, and if you really believe that, then you should be giving to him from your first fruits, not from what is leftover. Giving is not part of your discretionary spending—giving is subtracted before all other expenses.

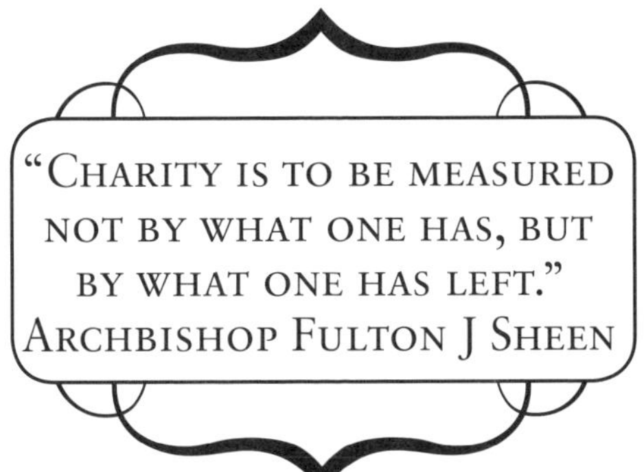

When you are figuring out how much to give, you are not calculating how much of your money you are giving to God. Rather you are calculating how much of God's money you need to keep. That's why we put giving first, otherwise, we can always find more stuff we want, or think we need, and when all of that is calculated, there is nothing left to give back to God.

Giving results in many blessings flowing back to the giver. Time and again, that principle is encountered in Scripture. For example from 2 Corinthians 9:6-8, we learn

Giving

"Consider this: whoever sows sparingly will also reap sparingly, and whoever sows bountifully will also reap bountifully. Each must do as already determined, without sadness or compulsion, for God loves a cheerful giver. Moreover, God is able to make every grace abundant for you, so that in all things, always having all you need, you may have an abundance for every good work." When we give cheerfully and with love, blessings come back to us in many forms.

Several couples we know have set up a "God's Account." It's money set aside each month in a special savings account specifically for the purpose of giving. The amount is budgeted and goes to their Mass offering as well as charities and non-profit organizations they support. Some of the money is used as God provides opportunities for it to be used. One couple tells us, "No matter how much money we give away, there is always money in God's Account when we are presented with an opportunity to give."

One of the most frequently asked questions in any discussion on giving is, "How much do I have to give?" In the Old Testament, they were required to give a tithe, which is ten percent. The Old Testament tithe was a way to support widows, orphans, the lost and the poor—those without standing as a person. This is the basis for our charity. However, using a percentage as a rule can turn the spiritual act of giving into just another bill to pay. The point is that your giving needs to be a faith response, not a way to follow some arbitrary rule. Giving must come from your heart, not your mind.

The Catholic bishops of the United States tell us the amount we are required to give is nothing. We don't have to give anything. "How much do we want to give?" is the question. Again, everything that we have is a blessing from God and we should give according to our means—which is a much more strenuous measure of our giving than an arbitrary percentage.

Chapter 8

So the ultimate decision on how much to give is between you as a couple and God. The two of you should have a discussion and take this decision to prayer. If you want to increase your giving, but do not see how it's possible, plan to add a certain percentage on a regular basis—maybe every quarter or every six months or even once a year. If you and your fiancé want to increase your giving, set specific goals and timeframes. God will bless you whatever amount you give if it is done joyfully in love and as a way to honor all he has given to you.

Insights

The ultimate decision on how much to give is between you as a couple and God. The decision should be made in prayer from a heart filled with love.

The Bible says

"Let not your hand be open to receive, but clenched when it is time to give." (Sirach 4:31)

Catholicism

"One of the most frequently asked questions in any stewardship educational program is 'How much do I have to give?' The answer (from a stewardship perspective) is nothing. We don't have to give anything. 'How much do we want to give?' is the question that stewardship asks. Stewardship is not minimum giving. It is maximum giving. That means giving as much as we can, as often as we can, from the heart as a faith response because we are generous stewards who want to share our time, talent, and treasure with others.

Giving

Frequently, in discussions of stewardship (or 'sacrificial giving'), reference will be made to 'the biblical tithe' (giving 10 percent of income) and other norms that could provide helpful guidelines for generous giving. As disciples of Jesus, each of us has a responsibility to support the Church and to contribute generously to the building up of the Body of Christ. The emphasis in the bishops' pastoral letter, *Stewardship: A Disciple's Response,* is not on 'tithing' (giving a fixed percent of income), but on giving according to our means. In many ways, this is a far more challenging norm. It challenges us to be good stewards not only in how much we give away, but in what we do with all our resources." (*Stewardship: A Disciple's Response Tenth Anniversary Edition,* p67)

Connect

1. What is your attitude about giving?

2. How much do each of you currently give individually?

3. What are your giving goals as a couple?

4. Complete the giving grid below to analyze where you are giving:

	LOCAL	NATIONAL	GLOBAL	TOTAL
Parish*				
Diocese*				
Other Catholic Charities				
Secular Charities				
Total				

*National and Global are shaded because giving to your parish and diocese is done locally.

Prayer Intention

CHAPTER 9

The Detailed Spending Plan

In order to develop a detailed spending plan you first need to calculate your *net spendable income*—this is the amount of money that is available for you to spend each month.

Start with the money that comes in—that's the big finger in the two finger economic system. Take your gross income, subtract your giving, then subtract taxes and other payroll deductions. The result is your *net spendable income*. Many people are surprised that giving comes off the top. As discussed in the last chapter, if you really believe that everything you have is a gift from God, then you should be giving to him from your first fruits, not from what is leftover. Giving is not part of your discretionary spending—giving is subtracted before all other expenses.

These calculations give you the amount of money available for the "little buckets" in your spending plan. Some typical spending plan categories are:

Saving/Investing	Housing	Food
Transportation	Clothing	Medical/Health
Education	Child Care	Personal
Vacation/ Entertainment		Debt Payments

When you are setting up your spending categories there is no right or wrong answer—you need to use the categories that are based on the way you spend and manage money. For example, if you have pets you may want to establish a pet category. Or if you have a hobby, you may want to set up a category for that. Do what works best for the two of you based on your discussion and agreements about how you will manage your finances.

A sample guideline spending plan is shown on the next page to give you an idea of how much of your net spendable income should be allocated to different categories. Everybody's spending plan is going to be a little bit different, so these are general guidelines. Take the guidelines and make them work for you. Look at your current spending and calculate your percentages to see if your spending falls into the low, middle or high range. It is best to be in the low to middle ranges. If you are in the high range in any categories you will have to cut back in other categories in order to have a balanced spending plan.

If you are high on most of the categories you will never have a balanced spending plan. It's time to get down to some serious cutting. If you are on the low side in most categories, you should have excess money to save. If you are in the low range and don't have excess money, then you are missing something. Your spending plan needs to add up to 100 percent of your net spendable income.

The chart on the next page can be used as a starting point for calculating the actual percentages allocated to your different spending plan categories.

Item	Recommended %	Actual %
Giving	10 – 15%	
Saving	5 – 10%	
Housing	30 - 40%	
Food	5 – 10%	
Transportation	10 – 15%	
Clothing	2 – 7%	
Medical/Health	5 – 10%	
Education/ Childcare	2 – 7%	
Personal	5 – 10%	
Entertainment/ Vacation	5 – 10%	
Debts	5 – 10%	

You will usually need several attempts to develop a balanced spending plan, so don't get discouraged if you have to go through this exercise multiple times. In developing your spending plan, use the data from your 60-day tracking, which should include cash purchases, checks written, purchases made using a debit card, plus anything you have charged or paid on your credit cards. The plan is to payoff the credit cards in full each month, so it is important to know what you are charging each month in order to build that into your spending plan. BUT if you have accumulated debt, you also need to pay that off so it is important that the debt payment is also part of your spending plan. You will discover more about debt payoff in a later chapter.

Why are we going through all of this effort?

Once you have agreed on where you want to spend money and have tracked your actual spending, the detailed spending plan provides a tool to help you to stick to your plan. I am sure you have had one of the same two following experiences when you were driving somewhere. Either you have no directions and are hopelessly lost or you have a map (GPS) of some sort and you have directions to follow. Having the directions always makes the journey easier and a spending plan is simply directions for money management.

A spending plan will eliminate overspending if you follow it. There is no more guessing about the next bill to come in or where you will get the money to pay it. It is important to build some 'fun money' into the spending plan—that's the same amount of money allocated to each of you that you can spend any way you want with no accountability. Obviously this needs to be a small amount that keeps your budget in balance, and each of you receives the same amount.

The plan gives you a framework for communication—you are talking about the same facts, not feelings or assumptions. The plan allows you to have fact-based discussions. Instead of saying, "You always spend too much money" you can say, "We overspent on entertainment by ten percent," which is a much more reasonable approach and makes discussions less emotional.

Once you establish the spending plan, you need to live by your spending plan. You just can't make up a spending plan and then stick it in a drawer and forget about it. Find a process that works for the two of you to track and manage your spending—it may be spreadsheets or an online tool or a financial software product. The process you use is not as important as using the same one consistently until it becomes second nature. Check out the tools and resources on the Compass Catholic website for spreadsheets that can help you develop your spending plan.

Your categories can be flexible—again define categories that work for the way you want to manage the details. However, your net spendable income—what you have left after giving, taxes and payroll deductions—is a fixed amount unless you find a way to earn extra income.

It is also important that you are both involved in the spending plan. Each person should have a role. Maybe one of you records the daily spending and the other runs monthly reports. You both need to be involved in monitoring the spending plan and making decisions. Plan regular "money dates" to talk about your plan, see if you are on track and make adjustments.

Your spending decisions need to be made based on your spending plan, not your checkbook balance. You may have money in the checking account, but if it is allocated to a category in your spending plan, you cannot spend it elsewhere!

Plan for the Unexpected

After you have established a viable spending plan and a way to track and manage your spending, there are two things you can do to prepare for unexpected events that are certain to ruin your spending plan.

One of the most important things that you can do is to establish an Emergency Fund. This fund will help you to pay for emergencies when they occur without having to put the bill on your credit card. Start by having $1,000 in short term savings where you can easily access it. And only use it for emergencies—the washer needs to be repaired or there is a major plumbing leak. These sorts of things happen often, and if you plan for them you can pay for them without ruining your spending plan. Life is a series of these unexpected events so it is wise to have an emergency fund to take care of them when they happen.

We've learned that $1,000 will cover most things. The key to success is to replenish the emergency fund as soon as possible after you use it so there is money available the next time you need it. As you become better and better at living your spending plan, grow the emergency fund to 3 months income, then 6 months income, and then, if possible, 12 months income.

You should also establish a "crisis budget" which is the topic of the following chapter.

Insights

Develop a Spending Plan that works for you and once you have it and are using it, build an emergency fund and a crisis budget.

The Bible says

"Everyone who listens to these words of mine and acts on them will be like a wise man who built his house on rock. The rain fell, the floods came, and the winds blew and buffeted the house. But it did not collapse; it had been set solidly on rock. And everyone who listens to these words of mine but does not act on them will be like a fool who built his house on sand. The rain fell, the floods came, and the winds blew and buffeted the house. And it collapsed and was completely ruined." (Matthew 7:24-25)

Chapter 9

Catholicism

"Temperance is the moral virtue that moderates the attraction of pleasures and provides balance in the use of created goods. It ensures the will's mastery over instincts and keeps desires within the limits of what is honorable. The temperate person directs the sensitive appetites toward what is good and maintains a healthy discretion: 'Do not follow your inclination and strength, walking according to the desires of your heart.' Temperance is often praised in the Old Testament: 'Do not follow your base desires, but restrain your appetites.' In the New Testament it is called 'moderation' or 'sobriety.' We ought 'to live sober, upright, and godly lives in this world.'

> To live well is nothing other than to love God with all one's heart, with all one's soul and with all one's efforts; from this it comes about that love is kept whole and uncorrupted (through temperance). No misfortune can disturb it (and this is fortitude). It obeys only [God] (and this is justice), and is careful in discerning things, so as not to be surprised by deceit or trickery (and this is prudence)." (*Catechism of the Catholic Church* 1809)

Connect

1. Define the categories you will use to manage your spending plan.

2. After defining the categories in your spending plan, calculate the percentage of your net spendable income allocated to each category.

3. What do you have to do to build an emergency fund of $1,000? 3 months income? 6 months income? 12 months income?

4. Discuss the process each of you is currently using to manage your spending and how you plan to manage spending as a couple.

Chapter 9

Prayer Intention

Chapter 10

Crisis

A crisis can turn our world upside down. It can be anything. At some point we will be forced to deal with the death of a loved one or friend. Most of us have experience with someone in our life being diagnosed with a serious illness—one day they are healthy and the next day they have a limited amount of time left to live. Then there are the natural disasters; fires, hurricanes, tornadoes, earthquakes, and floods. So many times, there is a financial impact when a crisis hits—usually through decreased income or increased expenses. The first way to survive a crisis is to get your financial house in order now. If you have your finances in good order, the crisis can be a little less stressful.

The second way to survive a crisis is to remember that God loves you. This helps you to stay focused and prayerful as you deal with the crisis. Keeping God at the forefront helps keep you from feeling discouraged, overwhelmed and forsaken.

Think about some crises stories from the Bible:

- Joseph's brothers sold him into slavery
- In a few hours, Job lost everything—his children, all of his financial resources, even his health
- Mary was a pregnant unwed teenager
- The widow almost had her sons taken into slavery to pay her dead husband's debts

Yet in each of the stories above there was ultimate good that came from the crisis:

- Joseph was able to provide for his family in a time of famine
- God appeared to Job
- Mary played a unique role in salvation history
- The widow learned a lesson about trusting God (2 Kings 4:1-7)

James 1:2-4 sums it up: "Consider it all joy, my brothers, when you encounter various trials, for you know that the testing of your faith produces perseverance. And let perseverance be perfect, so that you may be perfect and complete, lacking in nothing." God uses all circumstances, even difficult ones, for our ultimate good. We can use difficulties as opportunities to grow closer to God and learn things we could not learn any other way.

The third way to survive a crisis is to seek advice from Godly people who have been in the same or similar circumstances. They can be a great source of blessing and encouragement to you. You can learn from their experiences. They can tell you about resources they have used and even mistakes they made that you can avoid.

It is important to focus on one day at a time in a crisis situation. Matthew 6:34 tells us: "Do not worry about tomorrow; tomorrow will take care of itself." When you are overwhelmed, it's easy to get several steps past where you are, and worry about what's next. The important thing is to focus on the present and to not worry about the future. One day at a time. Sometimes, all you can do is one hour at a time.

In a stressful situation it is important to trust God. When we are praying for help, we expect God to resolve things in our way, in our time, exactly the way we want it to be resolved.

This just sets us up for disappointment and frustration, as God does not work according to our demands. It is important for us to trust him and believe in his divine providence without giving him deadlines.

Anger can be a common emotion during a crisis. You can be angry with the people you think caused whatever is going on—if you get laid off, it is easy to be angry with your boss. If you are sick, it's easy to be angry with God. This sense of anger at the situation can cause you to lash out at those closest to you, whether they had anything to do with your situation or not. But anger never solves anything and the Bible tells us to forgive "not seven times, but seventy seven times" (Matthew 18:22).

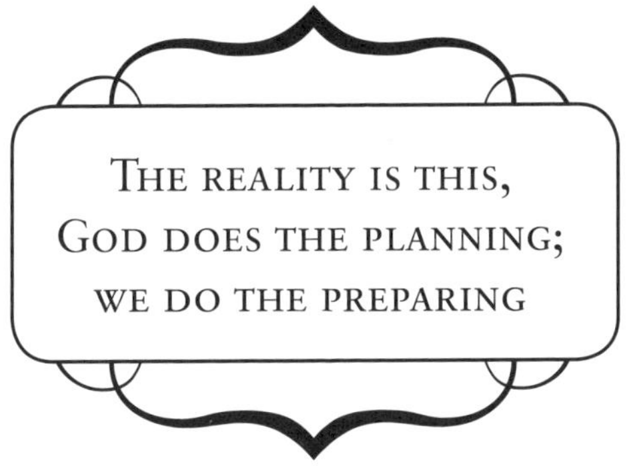

One of the things that we can do to in anticipation of a crisis is to prepare a crisis budget. This can be done in one of two ways. The first is to cut your expenses by a percentage —like 40 or 50 percent. The second way is to anticipate the most likely crisis and cut your budget to meet the circumstances of that crisis. Maybe there have been layoffs where you work and you have a vague sense that your department may be hit next. Or maybe your hours at work get cut in half. Look at the most likely things that may reduce your income significantly. Then develop a spending plan based on the reduced income. This can be as simple as noting which items in your current spending plan are "wants" not "needs." You can also rank the priority of items in your spending plan. If you have a crisis, you can easily cut out the lowest priority items.

Most times people will face the financial challenges in a

crisis by using credit cards to maintain their standard of living. This is very dangerous because you not only have a reduced income or increased expenses, but now you are adding debt payments to your expenses, PLUS interest, so you are just making the situation worse. We have seen many people use credit cards to sustain their lifestyle in a crisis and it just drags them down faster and faster.

The important thing is to know how much you spend on a monthly basis—that is the only way you can possibly be prepared financially for a crisis. Then you need to implement the crisis budget as soon as you anticipate the problem happening. For example, in most cases if there are layoffs at work, you can see them coming weeks or maybe months in advance. As soon as you anticipate the crisis, implement the crisis budget.

Anticipating and preparing before the crisis makes it easier to make objective decisions when the crisis occurs, instead of decisions based on emotion. Preparation will also help you have a sense of peace. One reason people don't plan for a financial crisis is because they really do not understand how much they are currently spending so they cannot anticipate any adjustments.

The crisis budget will not be fun to live and you will probably have to cut off all discretionary spending, but you will be in much better shape than if you did not have a crisis budget. The trick is to develop the crisis budget before you need it—when there are no emotions—and then use it as soon as there is a sense that a crisis may occur.

The best thing that can happen is that the crisis disappears and you have cut your spending for a few weeks or months, and you have saved money. The worst thing that can happen is that you entirely ignore the crisis and maintain your current lifestyle by using credit cards to replace the lost income. Many people have tried this method and have created significant debt that takes years and years to pay off. Having a crisis budget, whether you use it or not, can bring you a great sense of peace in a time of turmoil.

Sometimes a crisis is a blessing in disguise. It can help us grow closer to God, it can forge a stronger marriage, we can meet new friends through new circumstances or we can find a new path in life. From an unknown source: "Be thankful for the bad things in life—they open your eyes to the good things you weren't paying attention to."

Keep in mind this verse from Jeremiah 29:11: "For I know well the plans I have in mind for you—plans for your welfare and not for woe, so as to give you a future of hope. When you call me, and come and pray to me, I will listen to you." The crisis that you are facing, or might face in the future, is the opportunity to become more Christ like. God is always with us even when it's hard for us to recognize it.

Insights

Planning for a crisis can give you a deep sense of peace.

The Bible says

"There is an appointed time for everything, and a time for every affair under the heavens." (Ecclesiastes 3:1)

Catholicism

The wedding vows acknowledge that sooner or later we will experience a crisis: "I, (name), take you, (name), for my lawful wife/husband, to have and to hold, from this day forward, for better, for worse, for richer, for poorer, in sickness and in health, until death do us part."

Connect

1. Talk about developing a crisis budget. What are the most likely scenarios for a crisis and how likely are they?

2. Develop a crisis budget based on the most likely scenario.

3. Try living on the crisis budget for a month to see how it works.

4. If you are currently a two income couple, what life change may occur that would cause you to be a one income couple?

Chapter 10

Prayer Intention

Chapter 11
Debt

A dictionary definition of debt is "an amount of money that you owe to a bank, business or person." Debt includes bank loans, car loans, money owed to credit card companies, home mortgages, past-due bills, student loans, and money borrowed from relatives to name a few. Bills that come due on a regular basis, such as the monthly utility bill, are not considered debt if they are paid on time. Credit cards that aren't paid off at the end of the month are debt. Credit card cash advances are debt.

Cosigning is another form of personal debt. Do not cosign for any reason unless you are prepared to pay the entire amount you cosigned for. The Federal Trade Commission reports that as many as 75% of all cosigned loans end with the cosigner making payments on the loan. This is why the professional lender wanted a cosigner in the first place. When a person's credit score is low, the lender will try to get someone with a good credit score to cosign so that they have a guarantee that the loan will be paid. And here is the worst part. In many states the lender can sue the cosigner for payment after the first missed payment! When you cosign a loan you are personally taking a risk that the lender will not take.

Studies have shown that people who routinely use credit cards will overspend anywhere from twelve to thirty percent. Those little plastic cards just don't seem like real money!

Debt can be a burden—it often increases stress, which contributes to mental, physical, and emotional fatigue. It can stifle creativity and harm relationships. Many people raise their lifestyle through debt, only to discover that the burden of debt controls their lifestyle.

According to NerdWallet.com, the following figures represent the average debt of US households in May 2013:

Average credit card debt:	$15,162
Average mortgage debt:	$147,967
Average student loan debt:	$33,445
TOTAL:	$196,574

This is one time when it's good to be below average!

Would you be willing to go to the nearest pond and throw $101 into it each month? That $101 is exactly the amount of money you are wasting each month paying interest on the average amount of consumer debt—$15,162 at an interest rate of eight percent (which is a very low rate on consumer debt). With a higher interest rate or more debt, you are throwing away even more money each month. The $101 is the amount you have to pay in interest charges before any money goes towards paying the principal of the debt. Paying interest on credit card debt is a waste of money.

Oftentimes, people use credit cards because something is too expensive to buy with cash, so they decide to spend even more money to buy it with a credit card. Repeat—buying with credit often means you will pay twice as much for an item (the cost of the item plus the cost of the interest until the item is paid off).

Paying interest on debt enslaves you to the lender. Our plea to you is don't become a slave. Avoid borrowing money from any source. And it is especially harmful if you borrow from family. If you borrow from your family they may begin to judge the way you spend money, which often results in tension and hard feelings.

One of the ways to see the real cost of credit is to calculate the total amount you will pay if you put something on credit. Add up all the interest plus the principal and see how much that item will cost in total (not just the sales price), then decide if you really want to spend that much money for the item. This also helps you slow down and make a conscious decision, not an impulse buy.

Look at the chart on the next page and notice the interest rates. They are very realistic in today's economy. Assume you purchased a TV for $1,000 and put it on your credit card, and there were no other charges on that card. The next month after your purchase, the credit card company sends you a statement. You have a choice to pay them $1,000 or $20 ($20 is two percent of the balance). How long do you think it is going to take to pay for the TV at $20/month? In the right hand column, you'll see that if your interest rate is 22.9 percent it will take almost fourteen years. Over the fourteen years, you will pay about $3,338 for the TV. If you saw that same TV in the store for $3,300 would you buy it? Probably not! But we pay that much money when we buy items on credit and then only make minimum payments.

> SEEKING HAPPINESS IN MATERIAL THINGS IS A SURE WAY OF BEING UNHAPPY.
> —POPE FRANCIS

Look at the bottom section of the chart and assume you double your $20 payment to $40/month. This reduces your total time to pay off the TV from fourteen years to 2.9 years and the total cost (including principal and interest) drops from $3,338 to $1,374—a savings of $1,964! The time factor of money is key. By making more than the minimum payment, the interest charges were reduced significantly and the number of years required to payoff the loan was reduced by eleven years. Remember, when money is working for us, we want lots of time. When it's working against us, we want to shorten that up as much as possible.

Interest	**19.99%**	**22.99%**
Principal Borrowed	**$1,000**	**$1,000**
Minimum Payment	$20	$20
Time to pay off	9 years	13.9 years
Total Cost	$2,166	$3,338
Payment	$40	$40
Time to pay off	2.7 years	2.9 years
Total Cost	$1,304	$1,374

An easy way to think about the time factor of money is the Law of the Lowest—if you have to borrow money, always borrow the lowest amount possible, for the lowest time possible at the lowest interest rate possible.

To keep from throwing money away, here are our rules for credit card usage.

1. Use them only for budgeted items.
2. Pay off the balance in full each month to avoid paying interest and wasting money.

3. If you can't pay the full balance every month, use one of our tested and proven strategies:
   - **Plastic surgery**—any good pair of scissors will do. If you can't pay your credit card balance in total each month, cut them up!
   - **Heat 'em up**—put your credit cards on a sheet of aluminum foil on a cookie sheet, set the oven to 350° and put your cards in the oven for about 20 minutes. They shouldn't be a problem after that!
   - **Freeze your credit**—if you are really afraid of permanent fixes this might work for you. Put your cards in a plastic bag. Seal the bag. Put the bag in a bowl. Fill the bowl with water. Put the whole thing in the freezer. This strategy is for chickens as you can always thaw the block of ice if there is an emergency. But this method does make it very difficult to just grab your credit cards and head out shopping!

If you aren't supposed to use credit, how are you supposed to buy things? It's something that seems weird to most people—save before you buy it. The chart on the next page shows the difference between saving and paying the minimum amount on a credit card.

Our two couples from earlier are back. Couple One are the spenders and Couple Two are the savers. Couple One does not save anything—they spend their $20 each month. Couple Two saves $20 each month for fifty months.

After 50 months, they each decide to buy a couch for $1,000. Couple One buys the couch for $1,000 and is now $1,000 in debt. Couple Two buys the same couch by using their savings and still has $121 in savings.

	Couple 1 (Spenders)	Couple 2 (Savers)
50 months	Spends $20/month	Saves $20/month
Balance after 50 months	$0	$1,121
Purchase a couch	-$1,000	-$1,000
Balance after purchase	-$1,000	$121
For 13.9 years	$20/month payment	$20/month savings
Balance after 13.9 years	$0	$4,733 (@ 4.5%/yr)

At the end of fourteen years both couples have a fourteen year old couch, but by this time, Couple Two, who paid cash for the couch and continued to save $20/month, has almost $5,000 in savings. Whereas Couple One who has been paying the $20 minimum payment on the credit card has a net total of $0 in savings. By making the minimum payments, Couple One paid $3,336 for their couch—they threw away over $2,336 in interest and paid over three times more than the original cost of the couch! Sirach 20:12 sums up this situation: "There is one who buys much for little, but pays for it seven times over."

Pay off your Credit Cards

If you currently have any debt, you are obligated to pay it off. By borrowing the money, or charging purchases on your credit card you have agreed to repayment. In dire circumstances it may be permissible to settle a debt or declare bankruptcy but those choices need to be a last resort, after all other options have been eliminated. Bankruptcy is not an easy way out of debt.

Chapter 11

Pay your debt in full as quickly as possible. Once you have a complete list of ALL your debts (credit cards, car loans, student loans, loans from family, etc.) develop a Snowball Strategy. And here's how. Start by attacking your credit card balances first. List your credit card balances in order from smallest to largest, no matter what interest rate is on the card. Focus on paying off the smallest-balance-card first by paying any extra money you can afford against the card with the lowest balance. Make the minimum payments on all other credit cards.

You'll be encouraged to see the balance on that first credit card go down and finally disappear! After the first card is paid off, apply the payment from the first card plus the minimum payment from the second card to the second card. After card two is paid off, apply what you were paying on card one and card two to card three. That's the snowball in action! Once the credit cards are paid off, start paying off your other loans using the same strategy.

People sometimes ask if they should pay the card with the largest balance or highest interest rate first. Our experience is that paying off debt can be a long-term journey. By paying off the smallest balances first, you can see progress and stay enthused for a longer period of time. The short-term success will keep you motivated.

Insights

It takes discipline and two like-minded people working together and supporting each other to stay out of debt and pay off existing debt. With prayer and cooperation a couple can become entirely debt free.

Debt

The Bible says

"The rich rule over the poor, and the borrower is the slave of the lender." (Proverbs 22:7)

Catholicism

"Promises must be kept and contracts strictly observed to the extent that the commitments made in them are morally just. A significant part of economic and social life depends on the honoring of contracts between physical or moral persons—commercial contracts of purchase or sale, rental or labor contracts. All contracts must be agreed to and executed in good faith." (*Catechism of the Catholic Church* 2410)

Connect

1. Develop a complete debt picture for you as a couple by listing and totaling the following information:

- Creditor
- Total amount owed
- Interest rate percent
- Minimum monthly payment
- Payment amount you make monthly
- Date balance will be paid in full

2. Determine if your joint income is enough to cover your joint debt payments.

3. If either of you is making minimum payments on debt, calculate how much money you are paying in interest payments alone each month. (Use your statements to determine the amount of interest paid each month.)

4. Develop a snowball strategy for your combined debt and start by paying off your credit cards.

5. Determine if it is possible to eliminate any of your debts before the wedding.

6. If you are getting further into debt due to wedding and honeymoon spending, what can you do to eliminate or reduce this "newly wed" debt?

Prayer Intention

Chapter 12

Know Your Credit Score

It is important to stay informed about your credit report and your credit score. Each of you should get a copy of your credit report once every 12 months. To order a free copy, log on to AnnualCreditReport.com. AnnualCreditReport.com is the official site to help consumers obtain their free credit report. This central site allows you to request a free credit file disclosure, commonly called a credit report, once every 12 months from each of the nationwide consumer credit reporting companies: Equifax, Experian and TransUnion.

It is entirely your choice whether you order all three credit reports at the same time or order one now and others later. The advantage of ordering all three at the same time is that you can compare them. (However, you will not be eligible for another free credit report for 12 months.) On the other hand, the advantage of ordering one now and others later (for example, one credit report every four months) is that you can keep track of any changes or new information that may appear on your credit report.

Remember, you are entitled to receive one free credit report every 12 months from each of the nationwide consumer credit reporting companies—Equifax, Experian and TransUnion—so if you order from only one company today you can still order from the other two companies at a later date.

There are many websites which offer free credit reports. Be careful which site you use, as there many sites that offer "free" credit reports, but will charge you for other services. A good rule of thumb is that if you have to give them your credit card information, then it is not free.

Know Your Credit Score

You will be given an opportunity to purchase a credit score from any of the nationwide credit reporting agencies after you receive your free annual credit report from any of them. Unlike your credit report, which you can get at no cost to you, you usually have to pay for your credit score. There are certain instances in which you are entitled to your credit score for free, for example if you are denied a loan on the basis of your credit score.

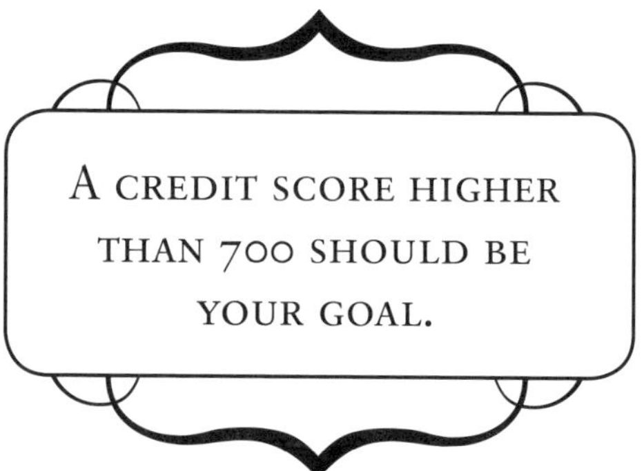

A credit score is a complex mathematical model that evaluates many types of information in a credit file. A credit score is a number designed to help lenders and others measure your likelihood of making payments on time. The score ranges from 300-850. Higher scores are better—scores above 700 indicate a good credit risk, while scores below 600 indicate a poor risk.

Credit scores are used by lenders to sift through your credit history instead of doing it manually, allowing them to make decisions more quickly and eliminating human error. Credit scores help companies decide to lend to you, hire you, issue insurance to you or rent to you.

The primary things that will harm your credit score are late payments or non-payments of bills and / or debts, bankruptcy, foreclosure, repossession, and bills or loans sent to collection.

Ways to improve your credit score are:

- Check your credit report to be sure it is accurate
- Reduce the amount of debt you owe
- Pay your bills on time

Chapter 12

Review your credit report regularly and report any inaccuracies to the credit bureaus to ensure your credit score reflects your actual credit history. The most common credit report errors are:

- Applying for credit under a different name (Robert S. Jones versus Bob Jones)
- An inaccurate social security number is used
- Clerical errors made when doing data entry from a handwritten application
- Loan or credit card information is applied to the wrong account
- Fradulent activity

Insights

Know your score and monitor your credit report on a regular basis.

The Bible says

"Take good care of your flocks, give careful attention to your herds; For wealth does not last forever, nor even a crown from age to age." (Proverbs 27:23-24)

Catholicism

"The Lord teaches us the path: not the path of poverty for poverty's sake. No! It is the way of poverty as an instrument, so that God may be God, so that He will be the only Lord! Not the golden idols! And all the goods that we have, the Lord gives them to us to advance the world, to advance humanity, to help, to help others. Today may the Word of the Lord remain in our hearts: 'Take care to guard against all greed, for though one may be rich, one's life does not consist of possessions.'" (Pope Francis—Vatican Radio 2013-10-21)

Connect

1. Sign up for a free credit report at: AnnualCreditReport.com

2. Share your credit reports with each other.

3. Determine if either of you need to take any action to improve your credit report(s).

4. Get a copy of your credit scores and share them with each other.

Chapter 12

Prayer Intention

Chapter 13
Major Purchases

Buying A Car

We all love that new car smell, but it comes with a high price tag. As soon as you buy a new car and drive it off the lot, the car loses thirty percent of its value through depreciation. That means the car is immediately worth thirty percent less than you paid for it. By the time you have owned that car for three years it is worth fifty percent of what you paid for it.

In order to keep your depreciation losses to a minimum, it is often best to purchase a reliable used car that is about 2 ½ - 4 ½ years old. Buying a pre-owned car is almost always more cost effective than buying new or leasing. But be sure to look at all your options—buying new, buying used, or leasing. Most of the time, buying used is the least expensive option, but sometimes it's not, so be thorough in your investigations.

Many times when we start thinking about buying a new car, it's because something broke on the old car. However, in most cases, the cost of repairing an old car is less expensive than the cost of buying a new car.

When you are thinking about buying a car, be careful that you are not reacting to a case of the "new car fever" disease. Buying a car is a decision on your mode of transportation. Don't use a car to define who you are.

When you are figuring out how much you can spend on a car, make sure you check the amount of money you have allocated in your spending plan for transportation. And remember that the calculation includes the car payment, any add-ons you may purchase—such as a sound system or window tinting—as well as the cost of insurance, which is usually higher on a newer car. You should also take into consideration the operating cost of the car. Buying a car that uses premium gas will increase your fuel costs if your current car uses regular gas; and remember to save a little each month to cover the costs of maintenance and repairs. In order keep your budget in balance, any car payments (if necessary!) should only equal half of your allocation to the transportation category. Insurance, fuel, tolls, and maintenance make up the other fifty percent.

If you are getting a car loan, be sure to calculate the total cost of the car over the life of the loan, including principal and interest. Many people just think about the monthly payment, but that monthly payment over five or six years can add up to twice as much as the car is worth.

One way to cut down on the amount of money you spend on cars is to retain your vehicle well past the loan payoff. If you pay off the car loan and take the same amount of money you were spending monthly and put it into a savings account, you will accumulate a down payment for a replacement car.

Buying A House

The American dream is home ownership, but as the recent financial crisis proved, that dream can quickly turn into a nightmare if you get in over your head. As with all your other spending, use the percentage guidelines in your spending plan to see how much house you can comfortably afford.

Most people secure a mortgage to pay for their house. A mortgage is a debt instrument, with the home (or real estate property) as the collateral. Mortgages are used by individuals to make large real estate purchases without paying the entire value of the purchase up front. The borrower agrees to pay the mortgage loan using a predetermined set of payments. Over a period of many years, the borrower repays the loan, plus interest, until he/she eventually owns the property free and clear.

In a residential mortgage, a home buyer pledges his or her house to the bank. The bank has a claim on the house should the home buyer default on paying the mortgage. If the borrower stops paying the mortgage, the bank can foreclose. In the case of a foreclosure, the bank may evict the occupants and sell the house, using the income from the sale to clear the mortgage debt.

Mortgages come in many forms. With a fixed-rate mortgage, the borrower pays the same interest rate for the life of the loan. The total payment does not change over the life of the loan. The amount of money applied to the principal and charged in interest changes monthly based on the outstanding loan balance. Most fixed-rate mortgages have a 15 or 30-year term. If market interest rates rise, the borrower's payment does not change. If market interest rates drop significantly, the borrower may be able to secure a lower rate by refinancing the mortgage. A fixed-rate mortgage is also called a "traditional" mortgage.

With an adjustable-rate mortgage (ARM), the interest rate is fixed for an initial term, but then it fluctuates with market interest rates. The initial interest rate is often a below-market rate, which can make a mortgage seem more affordable than it really is. If interest rates increase later, the borrower may not be able to afford the higher monthly payments. Interest rates could also decrease, making an ARM less expensive. In either case, the monthly payments are unpredictable after the initial term.

Other less common types of mortgages, such as interest-only mortgages and payment-option ARMs, are best used by sophisticated borrowers. Many homeowners got into financial trouble with these types of mortgages during the housing bubble years.

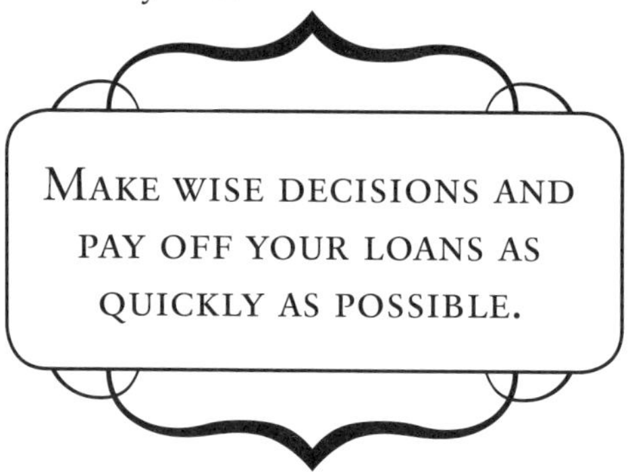

When buying a house, calculate the total cost, not just the mortgage. Be sure to include insurance, utilities, indoor and outdoor maintenance and many other costs that you might not think about. Often, your utility costs will be much higher in a house than they were in an apartment, and some utilities that may have been paid by the apartment complex may be your responsibility in a house. Before buying a house, be sure to calculate the total cost for housing, and if it is higher than your current housing costs, decide where you need to cut in other categories. You will quickly get into debt if your housing costs are significantly higher and you have not reduced spending in other categories. Remember you can only spend 100 percent of your net spendable income.

Also figure out what other purchases you will need to make related to owning a home. If you were renting a furnished apartment, and are moving into an unfurnished house you will need furniture. If you are moving from a 2-bedroom apartment into a 4-bedroom house, what are your plans for furnishing the other two bedrooms? In an apartment complex, all the repairs are taken care of by the management company. In a home, you will have to do the repairs yourself or hire someone to do them. And be sure to consider outside maintenance—lawn fertilizer, plants, a lawn mower, etc. All of these costs need to be included in your spending plan or you will end up running up debt on your credit cards to pay for all of it.

Make the largest down payment you can afford so you can get a lower interest rate on your mortgage. Having twenty percent equity in the house is key. If you do not have twenty percent equity in the house you will be charged PMI (Private Mortgage Insurance), which is one percent of the loan value and it lasts until your loan to equity ratio reaches eighty percent. Some loans require the PMI payment for the entire life of the loan. If you have to buy PMI, you are buying insurance to protect the lender in case you default on your mortgage.

If you are thinking about an adjustable rate mortgage, be sure you understand what may cause the rate to go up or down. How likely is it that your payment will decrease or increase? If the mortgage payment increases, it will impact your housing budget category and a significant increase may mean you will have to cut spending in other categories.

After purchasing a home, one of the ways many people get into trouble is by using home equity loans for renovations, loan consolidations or to supplement overspending. This is very dangerous. Understand that a home equity loan uses your house for collateral and if you default on the loan, your home may be taken away from you.

Instead of borrowing more, develop a strategy to payoff your mortgage as quickly as possible. The next few charts will show you an example of a $200,000, 30-year mortgage amortization schedule with an interest rate of 6 percent. Take a look at how much interest you would be paying during the first twelve months of the loan:

Look at the first year of the mortgage:

Month	Payment	Principal	Interest	Loan Balance
1	$1,199.10	$199.10	$1,000.00	$199,800.90
2	$1,199.10	$200.10	$999.00	$199,600.80
3	$1,199.10	$201.10	$998.00	$199,399.71
4	$1,199.10	$202.10	$997.00	$199,197.60
5	$1,199.10	$203.11	$995.99	$198,994.49
6	$1,199.10	$204.13	$994.97	$198,790.36
7	$1,199.10	$205.15	$993.95	$198,585.21
8	$1,199.10	$206.17	$992.93	$198,379.04
9	$1,199.10	$207.21	$991.90	$198,171.83
10	$1,199.10	$208.24	$990.86	$197,963.59
11	$1,199.10	$209.28	$989.82	$197,754.31
12	$1,199.10	$210.33	$988.77	$197,543.98
Totals	**$14,389.20**	**$2,456.02**	**$11,993.19**	**$197,543.98**

In the first twelve months you will have paid over $14,000 in mortgage payments, yet you only reduced the principal balance on your loan by $2,500. That means almost $12,000 was paid in interest. You want to get to the point where more money is going to the principal than to the interest.

Look at the last year of the mortgage:

Month	Payment	Principal	Interest	Loan Balance
349	$1,199.10	$1,129.44	$69.66	$13,932.27
350	$1,199.10	$1,135.09	$64.01	$12,802.83
351	$1,199.10	$1,140.76	$58.34	$11,667.75
352	$1,199.10	$1,146.47	$52.63	$10,526.98
353	$1,199.10	$1,152.20	$46.90	$9,380.52
354	$1,199.10	$1,157.96	$41.14	$8,228.32
355	$1,199.10	$1,163.75	$35.35	$7,070.36
356	$1,199.10	$1,169.57	$29.53	$5,906.61
357	$1,199.10	$1,175.42	$23.69	$4,737.04
358	$1,199.10	$1,181.29	$17.81	$3,561.63
359	$1,199.10	$1,187.20	$11.90	$2,380.33
360	$1,199.10	$1,193.14	$5.97	$1,193.14
Totals	**$14,389.20**	**$13,932.27**	**$456.94**	**Paid In Full**

Interest is calculated on the remaining balance. So in the last twelve months of the mortgage, your total mortgage payments are still a little over $14,000, but almost $14,000 is going toward the principal and only $450 is going toward interest.

By reducing the principal as quickly as possible, you reduce the amount of interest you pay, allowing even more of your payment to be paid against the principal. The following chart shows the amount of interest that can be saved over the life of the loan if you increase your payment to reduce the principal. If you make one extra payment per year, a thirty-year mortgage is paid off in 24½ years and you save almost $50,000.

To pay off the same loan ($200,000, 30-year mortgage at six percent) in twenty years, add $234 extra per month, and you will save over $87,000. And paying off the loan in seven years saves you almost half of what you would pay during a thirty-year payoff.

Year	Monthly Payment	Total Cost	Savings
30	$1,199	$431,676	$0
24.5	$1,299	$382,575	$49,101
20	$1,433	$343,887	$87,789
15	$1,688	$303,840	$127,836
10	$2,220	$266,400	$165,276
7	$2,922	$245,448	$186,228

Even if you can't pay a lot each month, every little bit helps. The next chart shows how much you will save and how many months you can take off this same mortgage by adding even a little bit to your monthly payment:

Additional Monthly Payment	Payoff Reduction	Savings
$25	1.7 Yrs.	$14,904
$15	1 Yr.	$9,195
$10	8 months	$6,108
$3	3 months	$1,858
$1	25 days	$644

Paying off the mortgage early and buying used cars may not be how our society tells us to live, but it follows the principles of how God tells us to live.

Insights

Save as much as you can for a down payment on major purchases, then pay them off as quickly as possible.

The Bible says

"Do not conform yourselves to this age but be transformed by the renewal of your mind, that you may discern what is the will of God, what is good and pleasing and perfect." (Romans 12:2)

Catholicism

"This willingness on the part of governments, communities, and individuals to live off debt means that people are 'living in untruth.' 'We live,' Benedict stated, 'on the basis of appearances, and the huge debts are meanwhile treated as something that we are simply entitled to.'

In fact, it's possible to go further and argue such attitudes reflect a mindset of practical atheism: living and acting as if God does not exist, as if the only life is this life, as if the future does not matter. Only people who have no hope—no hope in God, no hope in redemption, no hope for the future—will think and act this way." (Samuel Gregg, *Debt, Finance and Catholics,* Acton Institute, www.acton.org)

CONNECT

1. What debts do you currently have for cars or a house? How can you eliminate them?

2. Talk about your thoughts on buying used cars and keeping them for a long time.

3. How will you save money for a down payment on a house?

Chapter 13

4. If you own a house, what will you do to pay it off early?

5. List your financial goals for the next 3, 5 and 10 years. Share with your fiancé.

Prayer Intention

Chapter 14
Saving and Investing

When you make investment decisions, it is critical that you understand the time vs. risk horizon. Money that you will need in one to three years should be invested with little risk. Money that you anticipate needing in 5-10 years should have a low level of risk. Money that you won't need for twenty or thirty years can be invested in higher risk investments where one or two down periods won't create major issues as they might with investments needed in the short-term.

When you think of savings, think about it in three buckets. In the first bucket is your emergency fund (remember to start out with $1,000 and increase to three months, then to six months income, then twelve months income). This is short-term savings that has to be available for immediate conversion into cash. Your best options for this bucket are Money Market Funds, Short Term CD's, Treasury Bills, or a bank savings account. When you need to access your emergency fund, you have to get to it quickly so you want these funds in something that is safe and easily convertible into cash.

The second bucket is mid term savings—this is for larger ticket items that will take years of savings—maybe a college fund, renovating the house or replacing the car. Bonds or longer term CD's, which will pay a higher interest rate, can be a good options for this bucket. Mutual funds may be an option for this bucket, depending on how soon you anticipate needing access to the money.

And the third bucket is long-term savings, such as retirement or estate planning. This can be invested in real estate, stocks or mutual funds, which may fluctuate in value from year to year. When you average those fluctuations over a long period of time, the trend is likely to show an increase in your principal. If there is a downturn, there is time for recovery since you will not need to access these funds immediately.

To have adequate funds in retirement, you should save at least ten to fifteen percent of your income (excluding employer match). Pay your self first by saving a regular amount on a monthly basis. There are many options for retirement savings, such as pension plans, 401K, 403b, IRA, Roth IRA, etc. It is important to know what your employer offers. Many employers offer a match to your contributions. Be sure you are contributing enough to maximize the matching funds, otherwise you are leaving "free" money on the table. Many retirement plans have tax advantages, so consider investing in these accounts before investing in taxable accounts.

GOOD FINANCIAL PLANNING MAKES YOUR MARRIAGE STRONGER AND ALLOWS LOVE, TRUST AND CO-OPERATION TO GROW.

Keep the chapter on making wise decisions in mind when considering the perspective of the person who is giving you investment advice. Investment advisors make their money in different ways, so when you are dealing with an investment advisor understand how they get paid. By understanding how they get compensated, you can be comfortable that they are not pushing a product, which may not be the best product for your needs, but pays them the highest commission.

The fundamental principle for becoming a successful investor is to spend less than you earn and invest the surplus on a regular basis. In other words, be a steady plodder. Nothing replaces consistent, month-after-month investing.

Chapter 14

God warns us to avoid risky investments, yet each year thousands of people lose money in highly speculative investments and scams. How many times have you heard of people losing their life's savings on a get-rich-quick scheme? Sadly, it seems that Christians are particularly vulnerable because they trust others who appear to live by their same values. Avoid risky investments by praying, seeking wise counsel from your spouse, and doing your homework.

Saving for retirement

The following chart shows that if you start saving early it's not too difficult to save $1,000,000 for retirement. The biggest question is—will $1,000,000 be enough to live on when you retire? That will depend on your standard of living. In today's financial world most advisors will tell you that you will need approximately a minimum of 15 times your salary at age 65 in order to have enough money to last well into your 90's. Having a spending plan and knowing how much you spend will help significantly in determining how much you need for retirement and how much you are able to save on a regular basis.

Value after 10 years			
$$ Per Week	**5%**	**7%**	**9%**
$7	$4,706	$5,276	$5,865
$14	$9,412	$10,492	$11,730
$21	$14,118	$15,738	$17,595
$28	$18,824	$20,984	$23,460
$50	$33,745	$37,669	$42,183
$100	$67,490	$75,338	$84,367

Value after 20 years			
$$ Per Week	5%	7%	9%
$7	$12,458	$15,789	$20,244
$14	$24,916	$31,578	$40,488
$21	$37,374	$47,367	$60,732
$28	$49,832	$63,156	$80,976
$50	$89,638	$113,489	$145,859
$100	$178,737	$226,979	$291,718

Value after 40 years			
$$ Per Week	5%	7%	9%
$7	$46,505	$80,259	$143,763
$14	$93,010	$160,518	$287,527
$21	$139,516	$240,777	$431,290
$28	$186,021	$321,036	$575,054
$50	$332,180	$573,279	$1,026,882
$100	$664,361	$1,146,559	$2,053,765

When you are calculating how much you will need for retirement, keep in mind the Rule of 72. Take the number 72 and divide it by the interest rate you are earning. The result is the number of years it will take your money to double. If you have an interest rate of 8 percent, then 72/8 = 9. So your money will double in 9 years. If you have an interest rate of 3 percent, then 72/3 = 26. So your money will double in 26 years.

Chapter 14

Windfalls

Earlier in this book, you did an exercise to discuss how you would spend one million dollars. While it is highly unlikely that you will be given a gift of a million dollars, from time to time it is possible that you may get a small financial windfall. You may receive financial gifts as wedding presents, a bonus at work or maybe an inheritance. If you determine ahead of time how you will use the windfall, it will prevent arguments with your spouse and help you make wise decisions. You may want to allocate a certain percentage of any windfalls to giving, saving and spending.

Insights

Savings only happens if you plan it. Many people who appear to be wealthy because of their lifestyle do not have any savings, and people who seem to have a poor lifestyle can have a comfortable savings account. Diversify your savings into short-term, mid-term and long-term plans.

The Bible says

"The plans of the diligent end in profit, but those of the hasty end in loss." (Proverbs 21:5)

"Make seven, or eight portions; you do not know what misfortune may come upon the earth." (Ecclesiastes 11:2)

Catholicism

"When you are doing what you believe to be the will of God, that alone is enough to satisfy you and fill you with joy. When you are not, all the pleasures and possessions of the world are not enough to satisfy you." (The Dynamic Catholic, Daily Food for Thought, March 3, 2014)

Saving and Investing

Connect

1. How much savings do each of you currently have?

2. How will you be sure you have short, mid and long-term savings?

3. What are you willing to sacrifice short-term in order to have long term savings?

4. At what age do you want to retire and what does retirement mean to you?

5. What is your yearly goal for saving/investing (either a percentage of income or a dollar amount)?

6. Develop a plan for using financial windfalls.

7. Calculate how much money you will need for retirement (remember to factor in inflation).

Prayer Intention

Chapter 15
Children

During a recent *Night Line* segment, the interviewer met with children who wanted to be Hollywood stars and their parents. One little girl who had just turned six stated that her aspiration was to be a Victoria's Secret model so she could make lots of money and buy lots of stuff and then people would love her.

When the mother was interviewed, she agreed that the goal of her 6-year old daughter to model half clothed was a wise and moral choice of careers. Mom was every bit as enamored as her daughter about having lots of money so she could buy lots of stuff and then people would love both of them.

Surely this scenario cannot end well.

If finances are one of the most stressful topics about which to communicate, communicating about children comes in a close second. Add children and money to a conversation and you may have the perfect storm if you are not on the same page. Our perceptions about how to teach children are largely based on how well or poorly we were taught as children. We either want to imitate what our parents did or stay as far away as possible from what our parents taught us.

The most common mistake in teaching children about money is simply not planning as a couple how to do it. It is important for husband and wife to discuss and decide on what is important in your particular family when it comes to money management and finances.

Children

Proverbs 22:6 says, "Train the young in the way they should go; even when old, they will not swerve from it." The most effective way to "train a child" is to become MVP parents (*Your Money Counts Catholic Edition*, Howard Dayton, Jon and Evelyn Bean p127).

> The "M" stands for model. Parents must model the behavior they want to see in their child. Parents need to live the principles of generous giving, wise spending, getting out of debt and saving. What you do will deeply impact your children forever.
>
> The "V" stands for verbally communicating the financial truths from God's word. It's not enough for children to see you do something; you need to explain what you are doing and why you are doing it.
>
> The "P" stands for practical opportunities. It is important for children to experience first hand what you are teaching them. They need a chance to apply what they've seen you do and heard you say. And the more hands on these practical opportunities, the better. Practical opportunities allow them to learn through their failures and successes.

A young child (ages 3-6) can easily learn a lesson about waiting to buy something they want. Use opportunities when you are waiting in line at a store or in traffic to teach your children about patience so they learn to wait for what they want. This is a hard concept for people of all ages, and the earlier this lesson is learned the more it becomes a lifestyle.

Kids at this age need to learn that if they really want something, they should wait and save to buy it. The ability to delay gratification is a good prediction about how successful one will be as a grown-up. Set the tone when you shop—kids do not need a toy, candy or a gift every time they walk into a store.

This is also a good time to start a simple budgeting process. Use three jars or envelopes labeled "Give-Save-Spend." Every time they get money, some goes into each jar. The "Give" money goes to the offertory at church and/or another charity. The "Save" money is for more expensive items. Help the child set a goal, such as buying a special toy they want, but be sure it's not so pricey that they won't be able to afford it for months. The "Spend" money is for small purchases, such as candy or stickers.

Elementary school children (ages 6-10) need to learn how to make choices about spending. Find opportunities to help them make good financial choices. In the grocery store explain why you buy generic not name brand items because they cost less and taste the same. Give them part of the grocery list and have them make the buying choices, within the parameters of what you need, to give them the experience of making choices with money.

This is also the time to start teaching them about needs vs. wants. They may want the latest toy or game, but do they really need it? This lesson is easily tied to how you're making your financial decisions as a grown-up, asking questions like:

- Is this something we really, really need?
- Can we skip it this week since we're going out to dinner?
- Can I borrow it?
- Would it cost less somewhere else?
- Could we go to a discount store and get two of these instead of one?

Continue the simple "Give-Save-Spend" budgeting and the goal setting. If they are saving for a large purchase such as

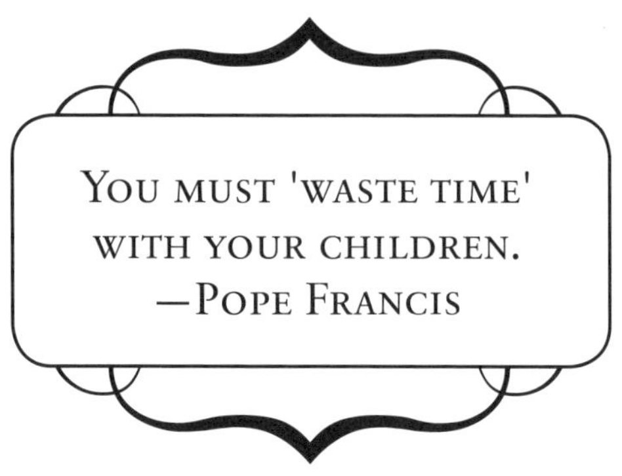

a bike, you may want to match what they save.

By middle school (ages 11-13) they are ready to begin focusing on long-term goals. This is the time to introduce the concept of compound interest, when you earn interest both on your savings as well as on past interest paid on your savings. Describe compound interest using specific numbers, because this is more effective than describing it in the abstract—see the "Compounding Your Return" calculator on the Compass Catholic Ministries website (CompassCatholic.org).

Help them think about how they are spending money regularly and the effect their spending may have on a long-term goal. For example, if your child has a habit of buying a snack after school every day, she may decide she'd rather put that money toward something that has more value to her personally.

In high school (ages 14-18) the goal is to help them be independent responsible spenders. At this age, their budget is more detailed and they should be managing their finances independently with a weekly parental review.

Whatever you do, don't bail them out—if they use their budgeted lunch money for a video game, then they need to figure out how to eat lunch the rest of the week without mom and dad giving them more money or making lunch for them. If you are providing money for certain items outside of their allowance, such as school clothes, have them do the shopping. They will shop and spend much more carefully if they make the purchasing decisions.

Chapter 15

Incent them to help save money. If they take the time to cut coupons and search for the best buys on grocery items or staples around the house, give them 25 or 50 percent of the savings as a reward.

High school is the time to start talking about college costs. Search for the "net price calculator" on college websites to see how much each college costs when including expenses other than tuition. Explain how much more college grads earn than people without college degrees, making it a worthwhile investment. Discuss how much you can contribute to your child's college education each year—be honest about what your family can afford so kids will be realistic about where they may apply. Have them look into financial aid, how much of it is "free money" such as grants and scholarships. How much will they need in loans and what government programs can help pay back those loans.

Parents are the number one influence on their children's financial behaviors, so it's up to you to raise a generation of mindful consumers, investors, savers, and givers.

Deuteronomy 6:5-7 says, "Therefore, you shall love the LORD, your God, with your whole heart, and with your whole being, and with your whole strength. Take to heart these words, which I command you today. Keep repeating them to your children."

As parents, we have the ultimate influence over how our children think. If we think that money and possessions are the ultimate goal of life, so will they. If we think that a lifestyle full of things will cause people to love us, so will they.

The world teaches children its way of handling money, which is contrary to God's way. We have the responsibility to teach children God's way of handling money. We must be even more intentional than the world in teaching our children.

Children

Our thoughts influence their thoughts. We can influence them toward the holy and moral or we can influence them toward the secular and worldly. We can help them see there is a better way or help them follow the path of the world.

How we train them determines in a large part their thoughts and attitudes when they are adults. Children can be taught to love things and use people or to love people and use things.

Insights

We can teach children to honor God or the almighty dollar.

The Bible says

"For the LORD sets a father in honor over his children; a mother's authority he confirms over her sons." (Sirach 3:2)

Catholicism

"The Christian home is the place where children receive the first proclamation of the faith. For this reason the family home is rightly called 'the domestic church,' a community of grace and prayer, a school of human virtues and of Christian charity." (*Catechism of the Catholic Church* 1666)

"Parents must regard their children as children of God and respect them as human persons. Showing themselves obedient to the will of the Father in heaven, they educate their children to fulfill God's law." (*Catechism of the Catholic Church* 2222)

Chapter 15

Connect

1. How did your parents teach you to manage money when you were growing up?

2. What was the best thing your parents taught you about handling money?

3. What will you do to teach your children how to handle money?

4. Will you give your children an allowance? What are the pros and cons of giving children an allowance?

5. Will your children be paid for chores around the home?

Prayer Intention

Chapter 16

Estate Planning

At the beginning of your life together it's hard to think about the end. But the end always comes and it is best to be prepared. Sirach 33:24 tells us: "When your few days reach their limit, at the time of death distribute your inheritance."

There are many things you can do to prepare for the unthinkable of losing your spouse. The information below is not comprehensive, but rather a starting point for discussions and planning.

The first step is for you both to have a complete understanding of your financial position—assets, debts, accounts and advisors. If you have been faithful in making a financial plan and keeping each other updated on the plan, this should not be a difficult task.

In the list of assets, include the following:

Tangible assets:

- Real estate
- Automobiles
- Valuable property (coins, musical instruments, antiques, etc.)
- List of online accounts, including website, user ID and password

Bank & Brokerage Accounts

- Bank accounts (savings, checking, money markets, etc.)
- Brokerage accounts
- 401K, Roth or other retirement accounts through your employer

Location of important documents:

Automobile titles	Business arrangements	Debt instruments
Deeds	Income tax returns	Insurance Policies
Leases	Military discharge papers	Mortgages
Power of Attorney	Trusts	Wills

It is also important that your spouse has access to a list of advisors. This list would include your: attorney, accountant, financial advisor, insurance agent(s), banker, and stock broker. The list needs to include not only their names but also the address, phone number, and email addresses.

It is important to have the right amount of life insurance, even though using it is an unpleasant thought. To estimate the amount of insurance you will need for income, multiply the required yearly income by twenty. This assumes the survivors will earn a five percent after-tax return on the insurance proceeds. Insurance coverage may also be needed to fund "lump sums," such as paying off debt or funding a child's education. Determine these needs and add them to the total amount of insurance. Remember, these estimates will be helpful to start a conversation with an insurance professional. Seek the counsel of an expert to determine your needs accurately.

The most important decisions you need to make are selecting the people who will make your health care and financial decisions if you are no longer able to make them. Be patient and pray about these appointments. They should be godly, responsible people who are capable of making wise decisions and have your best interests at heart.

Chapter 16

Health Care Power of Attorney (also known as a Medical Power of Attorney or Health Care Surrogate in some states) is an adult who will make health care decisions for you when you become unable to make them for yourself. The person you select must agree in writing to the appointment.

Based on your desires, which should be discussed while you are healthy, the person you appoint may withhold or agree to any type of health care, medical and surgical treatments, life-prolonging interventions, nursing care, hospitalization, treatment in a nursing home, and home health care.

Durable Power of Attorney is used if you become disabled or legally incapacitated. As with a traditional Power of Attorney, it names the person who is authorized to act on your behalf when managing your financial affairs. The person you have appointed must agree in writing to serve in this role.

Living Will (often called an Advance Directive) identifies the types of care a person does or does not want to receive in the event of becoming mentally incompetent during a terminal illness, or becoming permanently comatose. By stating in an Advance Directive that you want Catholic teaching adhered to, you can ensure that neither the agent nor the medical institution will disregard that teaching. Together they ensure that a trusted person, rather than strangers, will make circumstantially appropriate decisions, in keeping with the Faith.

Even though it is unpleasant to think about passing away (the good news is that we are going home to be with the Lord), you can give your loved ones a wonderful gift. When you have this information available for them, you communicate, "I cared for you in life and also now in my death."

Estate Planning

Insights

Planning for the end of your life may be unpleasant but it will be a great blessing to your spouse and your family.

The Bible says

"Seventy is the sum of our years, or eighty, if we are strong; Most of them are toil and sorrow; they pass quickly, and we are gone. Teach us to count our days aright, that we may gain wisdom of heart." (Psalm 90:10, 12)

Catholicism

"Death is the end of earthly life. Our lives are measured by time, in the course of which we change, grow old and, as with all living beings on earth, death seems like the normal end of life. That aspect of death lends urgency to our lives: remembering our mortality helps us realize that we have only a limited time in which to bring our lives to fulfillment." (*Catechism of the Catholic Church* 1007)

Connect

1. Make a list of your assets.

2. Meet with a lawyer for a will, health care power of attorney, durable power of attorney and a living will.

3. Become aware of the Church teachings on artificial nutrition and hydration and discuss with your fiancé.

4. Who will you designate as the guardian for your children if something were to happen to you?

Prayer Intention

Chapter 17

Forever

This book may have provided you with a different perspective on the role of finances in your marriage, or it may have confirmed what you already knew. Either way, as you start your marriage, we urge you to keep an eternal perspective. In his first letter to Timothy, Paul is sending Timothy a message about how to avoid the ways of the world and keep an eternal perspective. "Tell the rich in the present age not to be proud and not to rely on so uncertain a thing as wealth but rather on God, who richly provides us with all things for our enjoyment. Tell them to do good, to be rich in good works, to be generous, ready to share, thus accumulating as treasure a good foundation for the future, so as to win the life that is true life" (1 Timothy 6:17-19). The wealth of this world is fleeting and will never satisfy us for long.

Advertisements tell us to buy a newer, bigger, better what ever ... but money and possessions will never do all the things that the advertisers say that they can. Money and possessions will never bring you the peace you are looking for. It just won't happen, as true peace only comes from God. "Have no anxiety at all, but in everything, by prayer and petition, with thanksgiving, make your requests known to God. Then the peace of God that surpasses all understanding will guard your hearts and minds in Christ Jesus." (Philippians 4:6-7)

Moreover, money and possessions can't provide blessings. Proverbs 10:22 tells us, "It is the LORD's blessing that brings wealth, and no effort can substitute for it." And maybe the biggest things the advertisers say that money and possessions can provide is security, satisfaction and true financial freedom but they will never come from worldly wealth. We should be looking towards eternal life, focused on heaven—not on our worldly possessions—for security. Only God can provide the true blessings that will totally fulfill us. "Let your life be free from love of money but be content with what you have, for he has said, 'I will never forsake you or abandon you.'" (Hebrews 13:5)

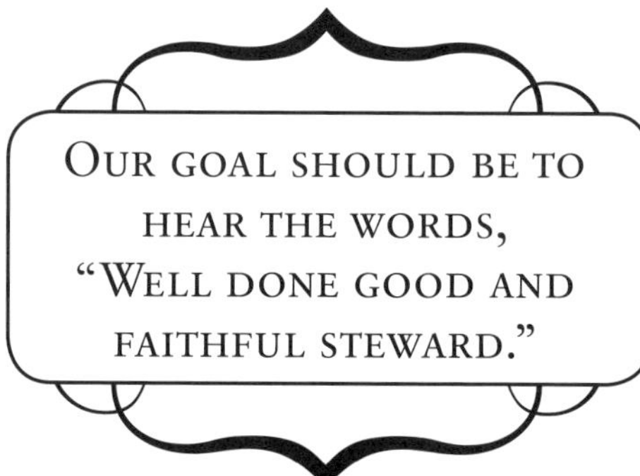

At the end of your life, when there is nothing left except your soul and eternity, do you want to hear these words from our Lord; "Well done, my good and faithful servant. Since you were faithful in small matters, I will give you great responsibilities. Come, share your master's joy"? (Matthew 25:23)

As you finish this book, we hope you have learned some things, and that you will use the Bible as a source of counsel. By planning wisely and communicating well and often, money and how you use it in your marriage can become a source of much joy and a blessing, not a source of conflict.

Please be sure to talk about all the open points that are left to discuss. If you don't resolve them now, they will come up later and later may be too late.

At the beginning of this booklet, we talked about two couples, both of whom had issues with money in their marriage. Couple One had financial challenges, which tore apart their marriage. After only a few years of married life, they are now divorced. Couple Two found a way to work through their money issues by learning what the Bible says. Today they are stronger as a couple, have a deep abiding faith and a solid marriage.

The question remains: **Which couple will you be?**

Prayer Intention

Our Prayer Intention for You

Dear Lord, we ask your blessing upon this couple.

Please help them keep you at the center of their wedding preparations and their marriage.

Allow them to become grateful stewards who carefully tend all of the gifts you have given to them.

Let them be open and honest with each other at all times so your light may shine on them.

Through you, may they recognize the traps of our culture and find grace and comfort in you alone.

Answer their prayer for assistance in finding Godly counselors grounded in your word.

Lord, may they be lavish givers who spread generosity wherever they go.

In each crisis they face, may they grow closer to you and closer to each other.

Permit them to understand and avoid the slavery of debt.

Assist them in making wise decisions in all areas of their lives through prayer and petition to you.

Help them to save and invest with an eternal perspective, understanding that only you can bring true peace and fulfillment.

May they teach their children how to be careful spenders, generous givers and wise savers.

And after a long and fruitful married life may they be united with you forever.

Resources

The Compass Catholic Ministries Bible study *Navigating Your Finances God's Way* will provide you with a deeper understanding of the topics in this booklet.

The Compass Catholic Ministries website (CompassCatholic.org) has many spreadsheets, calculators and other practical tools you can use for developing and managing your budget and finances. Follow us on Twitter and Facebook.

Bible References

God's Ownership	
Genesis 14:19	Psalm 50:10-11
Genesis 14:22	Psalm 82:8
Exodus 9:29	Psalm 104:24-30
Exodus 19:5	Proverbs 10:22
Leviticus 25:23	Jeremiah 27:5
Deuteronomy 10:14	Haggai 2:8
1 Chronicles 29:11-13	Acts 17:26-27
Psalm 24:1-2	1 Corinthians 10:26
Psalm 50:10-11	Luke 14:33
Psalm 82:8	1 Corinthians 4:2
We are Stewards	
Genesis 1:28	Matthew 19:27-29
Deuteronomy 30: 15-16	Matthew 25:14-30
Psalm 115:16	Luke 14:33
1 Kings 2:3	1 Corinthians 4:2
Isaiah 55:1-2	1 Timothy 4:4
Matthew 6:25-34	

Debt	
Deuteronomy 15:4-6	Proverbs 17:18
Deuteronomy 28:43-45	Proverbs 22:7
2 Kings 4:1-7	Romans 13:8
Psalm 37:21	1 Corinthians 7:23
Proverbs 6:1-5	
Counsel	
Psalm 73:24	Proverbs 11:14
Psalm 119:24	Proverbs 12:15
Proverbs 1:5-8	**Proverbs 19:20**
Proverbs 4:2	Proverbs 27:17
Proverbs 6:20-22	
Honesty	
Leviticus 19:11, 35-37	Micah 6:11-13
Deuteronomy 25:13-16	Matthew 15:19
Judges 17:6	Luke 16:10
Psalm 58:4	John 14:6
Proverbs 6:12	Acts 5:1-11
Proverbs 12:22	Ephesians 4:25
Proverbs 19:22	Colossians 3:9
Jeremiah 7:9-11	

Giving	
Exodus 34:26	Luke 11:42
Deuteronomy 15:7-11	Luke 18:18-23
Proverbs 3:9	**Acts 20:35**
Mark 10:17-22	2 Corinthians 9:6-11
Mark 12:41-44	1 John 3:17-18
Luke 3:10-11	
Foundation/Planning	
Proverbs 20:18	Luke 14:28-33
Proverbs 24:3-5	Hebrews 13:5
Proverbs 27:23-24	
Saving and Investing	
Proverbs 21:5	Sirach 25:3
Proverbs 21:20	1 Timothy 5:8
Ecclesiastes 11:2	
Our Culture	
Proverbs 11:28	Luke 12:13-15
Proverbs 23:4-5	Luke 12:22-34
Proverbs 28:22	Ephesians 5:3-5
Ecclesiastes 5:9-14	Colossians 3:1-2
Jeremiah 17:5-6	1 Timothy 6:7-10, 17-19
Matthew 4:8-10	James 3:14-16
Matthew 6:20-21	2 Peter 2:1-3
Matthew 19:16-23	1 John 2:15-17

Crisis	
Lamentations 3:19-23	James 1:2-4
Romans 8:28	Jeremiah 29:11
Isaiah 45:6-7	Philippians 4:11-13
Children	
Proverbs 22:6	Ephesians 6:4
Deuteronomy 6:6-7	Sirach 30:1-7
Forever	
Ecclesiastes 3:1-2	Mark 8:36
Psalm 39:5-6	James 4:13-15
Matthew 24:44	

Financial Dictionary

A complete version of this dictionary is provided on our website: compasscatholic.org.

Accrued interest

Accrued interest is interest that has accumulated on the principal balance of a loan, adding to the total amount owed on a loan.

Additional principal payment

Additional principal payment is made towards the principal balance of a loan. This can enable the borrower's future interest payments to be reduced. In amortized loans, such as most mortgages and auto loans, most of the early payments go toward interest. Making additional principal payments will pay off the loan more quickly.

Adjustable-rate mortgage (ARM)

Adjustable rate mortgages are a form of financing, secured by real estate, which carries an interest rate that may change over the life of the loan. The interest rate on an ARM is calculated by adding interest to a benchmark. For example "Prime plus 5 percent."

Amortization schedule

An amortization schedule is a table detailing the principal and interest for each payment due on the loan. The schedule differentiates the portion of payment that will be applied to interest expense and the portion applied to the principal after each payment.

Appraisal (real estate)
An appraisal is the estimated value of a property, based on an analytical comparison of similar properties.

Appreciation (real estate)
Appreciation is the increase in the value of property over time due to supply and demand, capital improvements, fluctuations in market conditions, inflation and other factors.

Asset
An asset is property or possessions owned by an individual or business that has monetary value. Includes real estate, personal property and debts owed to the individual by others.

Automobile Insurance
Automobile insurance (car insurance) is insurance purchased for cars, trucks, motorcycles and other road vehicles. It provides financial protection against physical damage and/or bodily injury resulting from traffic collisions. The specific terms of vehicle insurance vary with legal regulations in each state.

Balloon mortgage
A balloon mortgage requires a principal payment made at the end of a term to payoff the loan. For example, on a mortgage, amortization can be based on a period of years, but the loan terms require a lump sum or balloon payment at the end of 7 years.

Bankruptcy
Bankruptcy is the legal status of an individual (or organization) who is unable to pay their creditors. Bankruptcy is filed in a Federal Court. Bankruptcies are of various types. The most common is the 'Chapter 7 No Asset' bankruptcy that relieves the individual/borrower of his debts and liabilities. The borrower remains ineligible for loans for a period of time after

the bankruptcy has been discharged. The borrower is also required to re-establish the ability to repay debt.

Basis Points

A basis point is 1/100th of 1 percent. Basis points are used as a convenient unit of measure in contexts where percentage differences of less than 1 percent are discussed. The most common example is interest rates, where differences in interest rates of less than 1 percent per year are meaningful. For example, a difference of 0.10 percentage points is equivalent to a change of 10 basis points (a 4.67 percent rate increases by 10 basis points to 4.77 percent. An increase of 100 basis points means a rise of one percent.

Beneficiary

A beneficiary is any individual or legal entity, which is named as an inheritor of funds or property in a bank account, trust fund, insurance policy or similar financial contract.

Bond

A bond is a loan that's sold in shares as a security. Corporations and government entities (bond issuers) sell bond shares to raise money for special projects, expansion, or simply to cover budgeted expenses. One who purchases a bond is called the bondholder. The terms of the bond specify when and how the bond issuer will repay the principal to the bondholder.

Cancellation of debt

Cancellation of debt is the writing off of a borrower's outstanding principal balance, even though payment hasn't been made. The lender essentially wipes away the debt and the borrower is free from obligation.

Cardholder agreement

A cardholder agreement is the written statement of terms that governs a credit card account. The Federal Reserve requires credit card companies to provide cardholders with a cardholder agreement that defines the annual percentage rate, how minimum payments are calculated, annual account fees, and rights of the cardholder when billing disagreements arise.

Cash advance

A cash advance is a service offered by credit card companies where the cardholder can withdraw cash, up to a certain limit. Most credit card accounts allow for cash advances in addition to purchases, but the rates for cash advances are higher and the terms are more restrictive than those governing purchase transactions.

Cash advance fee

Cash advance fees are levied by a credit card issuer when the cardholder draws cash against a credit account. The fee might be structured as a per-transaction amount, or as a percentage of the amount of cash advanced.

Certificate of deposit (CD)

A certificate of deposit is a fixed-rate, time deposit issued by banks and other financial institutions. Upon purchasing the CD, the investor agrees to keep the funds on deposit with the CD issuer for a certain period of time. CDs pay higher interest rates than unrestricted cash deposits. Most CDs are FDIC-insured.

Closing costs

Closing costs are expenses incurred over and above the price of the property, by buyers and sellers when transferring ownership of property. They are of two types, non-recurring and pre-paid. Non-recurring expenses are incurred on items paid just once as a result of buying property or obtaining a loan. Pre-paid expenses are costs, which are recurring such as property taxes and homeowner's insurance. A lender usually gives the borrower an estimate of the total costs in a Good Faith Estimate within three days of receiving a home loan application. Closing costs normally include an origination fee, attorney's fee, taxes, amount placed in escrow, and charges for obtaining title insurance and a survey. Closing cost percentages will vary according to the area of the country and the lender.

Cosigner
A cosigner agrees to take responsibility for a debt if the borrower defaults. A loan applicant who does not qualify for a loan may be able to obtain financing if an individual agrees to be a cosigner.

Collateral
Collateral is an asset that acts as the guarantee in the repayment of the loan. The borrower may risk losing this asset if he is unable to repay his loan according to the terms of the loan contract or the mortgage or the trust deed.

Compound interest
For loans, compound interest is calculated on the total amount owed, including interest that has accumulated. Borrowers experience negative amortization when the principal amount of the loan actually increases because the monthly payments are lower than the full amount of interest owed. For savings, compound interest is calculated on the principal and interest paid previously that had been added to the principal balance.

Consolidation loan
A consolidation loan pays off and replaces several smaller debts. Debtors consolidate their debts to lower their monthly payment burden and overall interest rate. Consolidation loans are also called debt consolidation loans.

Contract
A contract is a written or oral binding agreement between two parties that is legally enforceable.

Conventional mortgage
A conventional mortgage refers to a fixed rate mortgage for a time period of 15, 25 or 30 years which is not insured by the government (FHA or Veterans Administration). In a conventional mortgage, the interest rate will not change during the entire term of the loan.

Credit bureau
A credit bureau collects and maintains debt payment histories of individual and corporate borrowers. Lenders use this information to evaluate a prospective borrower's creditworthiness.

Credit card
A credit card is a plastic payment card that's linked to a revolving credit account. The borrower/cardholder uses the card for payment, and receives an itemized statement of transactions at the end of each reporting period. If the balance is not paid in full by the end of the grace period, interest charges are added automatically to the account.

Credit check
A credit check is the review of a loan applicant's debt payment history. Lenders perform this review to predict how the applicant will handle the proposed debt obligations.

Credit history
Credit history is the documented and detailed statement of an individual's debts—including both debts that are open and debts that are fully repaid. Credit history is used to help the lender ascertain the risk and credit worthiness of a potential

borrower and whether he will be able to repay future debts on time. A married couple each has their own credit history.

Credit limit

A credit limit is the maximum amount of debt available to a borrower under a credit card, charge card, or other type of revolving credit facility. The borrower may apply charges to the account only up to the approved credit limit.

Credit report

A credit report is a documented statement of an individual's credit history and current credit standing. It is prepared by a credit bureau and used by lenders in determining the credit worthiness of the loan applicant.

Credit score

A credit score is a number that reflects the credit history as outlined in an individual's credit report (see also FICO score). A lender will calculate this number using a computer system as part of the process of assigning interest rates and terms to the loans they make. The higher the number, the better the terms that a lender will offer. A good credit score is around 720. It is possible to raise your credit score over time and by appealing incorrect items that appear on your credit report. It is smart for consumers to monitor and track their credit reports to ensure that the information is correct and to make sure that disputed items have been removed.

Credit worthiness

Credit worthiness is an individual's or business's ability and willingness to repay debt. When an individual or business submits a loan application, the lender reviews the applicant's qualifications, including credit history and income, and makes an evaluation regarding that applicant's credit worthiness. This evaluation determines if, and on what terms, the loan application will be accepted.

Debit card

A debit card is a plastic payment card that's linked to a deposit account. Debit cards are accepted for purchase transactions at participating businesses. When the card is presented and approved for payment, the transaction amount is almost immediately deducted from the account balance. Debit cards can also be used at the ATM for funds withdrawals, deposits, and transfers.

Debt-to-income ratio (DTI)

Debt-to-income ratio is the quotient of a borrower's minimum debt payments divided by that borrower's gross income for the same time period. DTI is used by lenders as one factor in the evaluation of risk associated with a debt request. From the lender's perspective, a higher ratio indicates greater risk.

Debtor

A debtor is an individual or entity that owes money to another. Debtors owing money to a bank or lender are called borrowers, and debtors owing money to investors (who have purchased the debtor's bonds or debentures) are called issuers.

Depreciation

Depreciation is a decrease in the value of property or assets.

Diversification

Diversification is a tenet of conservative investing. It calls for spreading out investment funds among different classes of assets, different industries, and/or different companies in order to reduce risk.

Down payment

A down payment is the initial and part cash payment towards the price of an item prior to the calculation of the loan amount.

FICO score

A FICO score is numeric value calculated by Fair Isaac Credit Organization that represents credit worthiness. When lenders talk about credit score, they're usually referring to the FICO. The FICO score is calculated by a proprietary algorithm that considers an individual's payment history, debt level, and other related factors.

Financial planner

A financial planner is a qualified professional who helps individuals and businesses set financial targets and take the appropriate steps to meet those targets. An individual may seek the services of a financial planner when starting an investment program or when planning for retirement.

First mortgage

A first mortgage receives the primary position amongst all loans taken out against a property. In case of the borrower defaulting, it is claimed first.

Fixed-rate mortgage (FRM)

A fixed-rate mortgage is loan secured by real estate property that accrues interest at the same rate throughout the life of the loan.

Flood insurance

The national flood insurance program denotes specific insurance to protect against property loss from flooding. In certain flood prone areas, the federal government requires flood insurance to secure mortgage loans backed by federal agencies such as the FHA and VA. Flood insurance is a separate policy from homeowner's insurance and is administered by FEMA.

Health Insurance

Health insurance covers the risk of incurring medical expenses. According to the Health Insurance Association of America, health insurance is defined as coverage that provides for the payments of benefits as a result of sickness or injury. It includes insurance for losses from accident or medical expense.

Homeowner's insurance

Homeowners insurance is a form of property insurance that is designed to protect an individual's home from damages to the house itself or to possessions in the home. It also covers personal liability and theft.

Interest

Interest is money paid by the borrower to the lender for the use of the money, calculated as a percentage of the money borrowed and paid over a specified time. For saving and investing, interest is money paid to the saver or investor for use of the money.

Investment income

Investment income is the gross income from property held for investment such as interest, dividends, annuities and royalties.

IRA (Individual Retirement Account)

An IRA allows individuals to deduct pretax income, up to specific annual limits, toward savings for retirement. Contributions to the traditional IRA may be tax-deductible depending on the taxpayer's income, tax filing status and other factors.

Joint account

A joint account is owned by two or more persons who share in the rights and liabilities of the account.

Joint credit

Joint credit issued to a couple based on both of their incomes, credit reports, and assets.

Joint liability

Joint liability is two or more people assuming responsibility to repay debt.

Joint tenants (with right of survivorship)

Joint tenants are two or more people who own a home, either as a joint tenants or tenants in common. Each individual owns a share (or interest) of the entire property. This means that specific areas of the house are not owned by any one individual, but instead, are shared as a whole. When a property is owned by joint tenants, the property automatically gets transferred to the remaining surviving owner(s) upon a joint tenant's death.

Late payment fee

A late payment fee is charged to the borrower for not making the payment on time.

Line of credit

A line of credit is the maximum amount a financial institution is committed to lend to a borrower during a designated time period.

Liquid assets

Liquid assets can be quickly converted into cash such as bank accounts, CD's, or bonds.

Loan origination fee

A loan origination fee is assessed by the lender for underwriting a loan. This fee covers the time and preparation associated with the inception of a new loan.

Market value

Market value is the highest price a willing buyer would pay and a willing seller would accept, both being fully informed, and the property being for sale for a reasonable time period.

MLS (Multiple Listing Service)
Multiple Listing Service is a suite of services used by real estate professionals to share information about property for sale.

Money market deposit account
A money market deposit account is offered by banks or credit unions, so it is FDIC insured. There is usually a minimum deposit amount and a limit on the number of monthly withdrawals.

Money market mutual fund
A money market mutual fund is offered by investment companies, which invest in short term paper debts, designed to produce high yields without the loss of capital. Not FDIC insured.

Mortgage
A mortgage is a debt instrument secured by real estate property. The terms mortgage loan and mortgage are used interchangeably.

Mortgage debt
Mortgage debt is the outstanding principal on a loan that's backed by residential real estate collateral.

Mortgage insurance (PMI)
Mortgage insurance protects lenders against defaults or losses from a borrower. Borrowers are required to carry Private Mortgage Insurance if their loan has loan-to-value ratio higher than 80 percent. Depending on the type of loan, the borrower will have to pay an initial premium and a monthly payment. The monthly payment will continue until the equity of the home is greater than 20 percent. Some mortgages may require mortgage insurance over the life of the loan.

Mortgage Loan

A mortgage loan is a debt instrument secured by real estate property. The terms mortgage loan and mortgage are used interchangeably.

Mortgage refinance

A mortgage refinance is the option to pay off an old mortgage loan with a new one. This typically saves the borrower money in terms of a lower interest rate on the new loan.

Mutual fund

A mutual fund is a professionally managed portfolio of securities that builds capital by selling shares to investors. Mutual funds give the individual investor access to a diversified, regulated portfolio. The fund publishes its investment strategy and objective along with its historic performance in a prospectus. Gains or losses in the portfolio are shared by the shareholders/investors.

Negative amortization

Negative amortization occurs when the interest due on the loan is more than the monthly interest payments. The unpaid interest is added to the principal balance of the loan. In a negative amortization, the loan of the borrower increases and thus he ends up owing more than the original loan.

Negative equity

Negative equity occurs when the value of an asset securing a loan dips below the loan balance. For example, an individual could take out a mortgage loan to finance 100 percent of a home purchase. If the home's value subsequently drops, (for example, due to recession) the homeowner would have negative equity. Selling the home would require the homeowner to pay out of pocket to cover the difference between the sales price and the loan balance.

Net worth

Net worth is the total sum of all of assets minus all debts. Assets include home, car, investments, etc. Debts include mortgages, car loans, credit cards balances, and other loans.

POA (Power of Attorney)

Power of attorney is a legal document that authorizes one person to act on behalf of another. There can be a general POA, granting complete authority or a specific POA for a specific act or a certain period of time.

Principal

Principal is the actual value of a mortgage or loan or the balance left on a loan, not taking into account any future interest.

Principal, interest, taxes, insurance (PITI)

Principal, interest, taxes and insurance are different parts of a complete mortgage payment. Principal is the amount applied to the debt balance, interest is the monthly-accrued financing charge, taxes are pro-rated amounts applied to the annual tax bill, and insurance is the pro-rated amount for the homeowner's and/or mortgage insurance premiums.

Private mortgage insurance (PMI)

Private mortgage insurance protects lenders against defaults or losses from a borrower. Borrowers are required to carry Private Mortgage Insurance if their loan-to-value ratio is higher than 80 percent. Depending on the type of loan, the borrower will have to pay an initial premium and a monthly payment. The monthly payment will continue until the equity of the home is greater than 20 percent. Some mortgages may require mortgage insurance over the life of the loan.

Property tax

Property tax is assessed by the state or local government on real estate and personal property. Amount varies depending on the property's value and the various services provided to the property. Property taxes are most commonly paid into an escrow account and the lender is responsible for paying the tax bill when it is due.

Roth IRA

A Roth IRA is a type of tax advantaged retirement savings account available in the US. Contributions to a Roth IRA are made with after tax money, but earnings and qualified withdrawals are tax-free. Qualified withdrawals cannot be made until the account has been opened for five years or the account holder reaches age 59-1/2. Roth IRA's are subject to income and annual contribution limits.

Rule of 72

The rule of 72 is a means of estimating how many years it will take to double an investment earning a certain interest rate. To make the calculation, divide the number 72 by the compound interest rate. For example, a 10 percent interest rate will double an investment in approximately 7.2 years.

Savings account

A savings account is a bank or credit union deposit that earns interest and can be withdrawn on demand.

Second mortgage

A second mortgage is a mortgage made subordinate to the first one. In bankruptcy, the lenders of the second mortgage are paid after the first mortgage is paid in full.

Secured debt

A secured debt is a loan that's supported by collateral. Mortgages are secured because the lender takes a lien on the property and has the right to foreclose in a default situation. Auto loans are also secured because the lender takes a lien on the vehicle.

Umbrella insurance

Umbrella insurance refers to liability insurance that is in addition to other policies. Umbrella policies are usually made in addition to a homeowners and automobile insurance. The term "umbrella" refers to the broad coverage of the policy.

Variable rate mortgage

A variable rate mortgage has an interest rate which changes periodically based on a financial index. Also referred to as an adjustable-rate mortgage.

Will

A will is a legally binding document in which an individual specifies how he would like his property distributed after his death. The will can also specify a guardian for dependents and an executor for the estate.